"This book shortens the learning curv[...] ?R careers. Given the rapid pace of chang[...] narketing disciplines this can be the d[...] d 'truly thriving' in one's career [...]
[...]O Worldwide

"Succeeding in today's pro[...] especially the modern PR agency is both challengin[...]ng. Society and business are now digital customers and emp[...] driving the relationship and the conversation, meaning that agen[...]s must be providing ideas and solutions at a much greater pace. As such, professionals in those firms need to understand the nuances of firm life. *How to Succeed in a PR Agency* is a must-read to map out your individual path to success."
            —Gary F. Grates, Principal, W2O Group

"This book's emphasis on business acumen and client relationship management makes it an ideal learning resource for public relations students and young professionals. The authors' real-world experience and insights from industry leaders are organically blended with a realistic and reliable roadmap for launching a successful career in a PR agency."
        —Yan Jin, Ph.D., Professor of Public Relations, Grady College of
            Journalism and Mass Communication, University of Georgia

"Every would-be PR agency professional should read this book! You'll learn what usually takes a few years of working at an agency about the 101 on PR agency life, including its architecture and operation, managing your career, the importance of team and team building, managing client relationships, the adrenaline rush of new business pitches and more. I'm surprised that a book like this hasn't been written before but, thankfully, now it has."
        —Patrice Tanaka, Founder and Chief Joy Officer, Joyful Planet, and
                co-founder three award-winning PR agencies

How to Succeed in a PR Agency

Learning how to be successful in a public relations (PR) agency is a stressful on-the-job, sink-or-swim, immersive experience. While other texts teach PR theory and practice, no other book guides early to mid-career PR professionals through the day-to-day life of working in an agency and the skills required to excel and build a career.

This text demystifies the PR agency experience with foundational information to simplify and clarify agency life. Authors Kristin Johnson and Shalon Roth, who each grew successful careers in PR agencies, share secrets that no one will teach in a class or a seminar. This is real talk about real life in an agency – punctuated by anecdotes from leaders in the industry. This is a must-read for communications students and PR professionals looking to grow their career and become indispensable to teams and clients.

Kristin Johnson works as a client advisor and executive coach at Logos Consulting Group and Logos Institute for Crisis Management and Executive Leadership, and is an adjunct instructor at New York University in the School of Professional Studies (NYU-SPS), where she has taught in the master's level public relations and corporate communications program since 2014. Kristin also serves as a mentor and judge for NYU Stern's W. R. Berkley Innovation Labs $300K Entrepreneurs Challenge, which aims to develop people and ideas that create value for business and society.

Shalon Roth has spent the last 15 years on the front lines of PR and communications agencies serving start-ups to multinational publicly traded companies. She founded PR-it®, which combines the power of a proprietary data-driven pricing model with a global community of high-caliber, seasoned public relations, digital and creative experts to deliver high-quality projects to brands, and on-demand support to agencies managing workflow peaks.

How to Succeed in a PR Agency

Real Talk to Grow Your Career & Become Indispensable

Kristin Johnson and Shalon Roth

Routledge
Taylor & Francis Group
NEW YORK AND LONDON

First published 2019
by Routledge
52 Vanderbilt Avenue, New York, NY 10017

and by Routledge
2 Park Square, Milton Park, Abingdon, Oxon, OX14 4RN

Routledge is an imprint of the Taylor & Francis Group, an informa business

© 2019 Taylor & Francis

The right of Kristin Johnson and Shalon Roth to be identified as authors of this work has been asserted by them in accordance with sections 77 and 78 of the Copyright, Designs and Patents Act 1988.

All rights reserved. No part of this book may be reprinted or reproduced or utilised in any form or by any electronic, mechanical, or other means, now known or hereafter invented, including photocopying and recording, or in any information storage or retrieval system, without permission in writing from the publishers.

Trademark notice: Product or corporate names may be trademarks or registered trademarks, and are used only for identification and explanation without intent to infringe.

Library of Congress Cataloging in Publication Data
Names: Johnson, Kristin (Public relations consultant), author. | Roth, Shalon, author.
Title: How to succeed in a PR agency : real talk to grow your career & become indispensable / Kristin Johnson, Shalon Roth.
Description: New York, NY : Routledge, 2019. | Includes index.
Identifiers: LCCN 2018035105 | ISBN 9781138352674 (hardback) | ISBN 9781138352681 (pbk.)
Subjects: LCSH: Public relations—Vocational guidance. | Public relations firms.
Classification: LCC HD59.J595 2019 | DDC 659.2023—dc23
LC record available at https://lccn.loc.gov/2018035105

ISBN: 9781138352674 (hbk)
ISBN: 9781138352681 (pbk)
ISBN: 9780429434624 (ebk)

Typeset in Bembo
by Swales & Willis Ltd, Exeter, Devon, UK

This book is dedicated to the next generation of communication professionals. May you use your PR powers for good!

Contents

Acknowledgments   xi
About the Authors   xiii

PART I
Why Indispensable?   **1**

1. About This Book   3
2. Who Is This Book For?   4
3. What's in It for You?   5

PART II
Agency Basics   **7**

4. Architecture of Agency Life   9
5. The Life Cycle of Business   16
6. Money Honey   29
7. Budget Basics   37
8. Staffing   45
9. Ethical Conduct   53
10. Writing Essentials   58

PART III
Forget Titles   **65**

11. A Leader at Every Level   67
12. Achieving Authenticity   72
13. Diplomacy and Persuasion   80
14. Managing Expectations   86
15. PR: Personal Relationships   92

PART IV
Lead the Way   99

16 Building a Team	101
17 Personal Branding	113
18 Managing Your Career	120
19 Managing the Careers of Others	127
20 Managing Client Relationships	133

PART V
Pay It Forward   139

21 A Message from the Authors	141
List of Contributors	143
Index	144

Acknowledgments

We would like to thank our wonderful Routledge editorial partners, Ross Wagenhofer and Nicole Salazar, for believing in our project and being an absolute delight to work with. We would also like to thank the wider Routledge team for all their hard work in bringing this book to life.

A huge thanks is also due to our fantastic group of contributors who have enriched this book by providing diverse perspectives across sectors, functions, and geographies. We would also like to thank the Public Relations Society of America (PRSA) and Forty2 for allowing us to use their words of wisdom.

From Kristin

Thank you to Shalon Roth, my co-author, for working with me to create this much-needed book. To my teacher, mentor, friend, and boss, Helio Fred Garcia, who motivated me to write this book and gifted me time to make it happen – thank you. I hope this book shapes and inspires the paths of many public relations (PR) professionals in your honor. Many thanks also go to my family (hi mom and dad!) and my extended Logos family, Barbara Greene, Anthony Ewing, Adam Tiouririne, Holly Helstrom, Yinnan Shen, Raleigh Mayer, and Katie Garcia, who supported me. To the nearly 200 students who've taken my elective class at NYU – thank you for your time, your trust, and for the lessons you shared with me. Whether you know it or not, you helped write this book. To the special leaders who gave me opportunity and provided guidance that drove my career and understanding of public relations, thank you Nancy Turett, Jill Dash, Toni Muzi Falconi, John Doorley, Lauren Letellier, and Anne Woodbury. To my countless former PR agency colleagues and clients, many of whom I count as friends today and many of whom are named as contributors in this book – thank you for sharing everything from outrageous disappointment to blockbuster success. PR is definitely a team sport. And to my husband Carl Henningson, thank you for your love, encouragement, and support. For the record, I'm the lucky one.

From Shalon

I'd like to thank my co-author, Kristin Johnson – I'm so glad we made this book happen! Special thanks are also due to Jason Courtmanche, my high-school English teacher who taught me everything I know about writing. I'd also like to thank all the fantastic bosses, colleagues, and clients who have been an inspiration and taught me incredible things over the years. I'm grateful for your energy, humor, collaboration, and trust, which never wavered whether things were going swimmingly or about to hit the fan. I'd also like to thank all of the worst people I've ever worked with – you've taught me so much about integrity, kindness, and resilience. Often the most difficult experiences are the best teachers. I'd like to express my deepest gratitude to my husband, James Kerr, for believing in me unconditionally and providing the ideal situation for me to pursue my professional dreams – your love and support is the greatest gift I've ever received. I'd also like to thank my family and friends for their ongoing encouragement, especially Mike and Lauri Roman who have treated me like their own daughter for the last two decades.

About the Authors

Kristin Johnson helps those she works with find ease in burden, order in chaos, and imagination where there is ordinary. She is based in New York City but works with clients around the USA and around the world.

Within Logos, Kristin serves as senior vice president and chief operating officer to manage and expand business operations, as well as to oversee and develop leadership initiatives within the firm to ever advance Logos learning and service to clients.

In her client work, Kristin helps business executives, technical experts, healthcare providers, and others to build and strengthen their leadership capacity in career defining moments using strategic thinking and effective communication. She specializes in helping technical experts simplify the complicated and clarify the complex while maintaining the heart of their content. She works with clients both individually and in groups to support the effective delivery of meaningful messages in times of calm and in times of crisis. Her work spans multiple sectors, including finance, fashion, start-ups and non-governmental organizations (NGOs), but she has a special passion for and deep experience with the many facets of healthcare communication.

In addition to her roles at Logos, Kristin is an adjunct instructor at New York University in the School of Professional Studies (NYU-SPS), where she has taught in the master's level public relations and corporate communications program since 2014. Kristin also serves as a mentor and judge for NYU Stern's W. R. Berkley Innovation Labs $300K Entrepreneurs Challenge, which aims to develop people and ideas that create value for business and society.

Kristin has worked at several leading global public relations (PR) firms, including Edelman, TogoRun (an Omnicom Company) and Biosector 2 (an inVentiv Health Company), where she managed annual and project-based PR activities for branded and unbranded consumer, product, and business-to-business campaigns. In addition, Kristin has provided US and non-US based clients with strategic counsel on corporate communication efforts including issues and crisis management, social media identity development, corporate policy, thought leadership, and stakeholder communication.

Kristin holds an Investment Foundations Certificate from the CFA Institute. She earned a Master of Science degree in public relations and corporate communications at New York University and graduated with dual Bachelor of Arts degrees in communication arts and Spanish from the University of Wisconsin in Madison, Wisconsin.

Shalon Roth has spent the last 15 years on the front lines of PR and communications agencies serving start-ups to multinational publicly traded companies. She founded PR-it®, which combines the power of a proprietary data-driven pricing model with a global community of high-caliber, seasoned public relations, digital and creative experts to deliver high-quality projects to brands and on-demand support to agencies managing workflow peaks.

Before inspiration struck to go out on her own, Shalon worked brand-side as the executive vice president of corporate communications and public affairs for the C-suite of a biotechnology company that she consulted for 10 years prior.

Shalon met her co-author Kristin Johnson at TogoRun (an Omnicom Company) while working on the conglomerate's largest account. She also worked at Biosector 2 (a Syneos Health Company, formerly inVentiv Health) as a strategist on global accounts in the New York and London offices where she oversaw disease awareness campaigns, market research, data communications, reputation management, and commercial consulting projects.

At Biosector 2, Shalon became known for her quality-control protocols that grew a single-brand account from a £200,000 piece of business into a multi-million-pound global franchise within two years. She also served on the management team where she trained and mentored most of the agency's staff.

Shalon started her career as the fifth employee at Ricochet PR, a media relations agency in New York City focused on technology clients. After joining the executive team in her early twenties, she founded the healthcare and industrial sciences divisions, helping to grow the firm to over 50 employees and millions in revenues.

Shalon graduated from New York University with an honors Bachelor of Science degree in communications. She currently lives in London with her husband, where she enjoys frequent medieval castle visits and alpaca walks in her spare time.

Part I
Why Indispensable?

1 About This Book

> Everything you do or say is public relations.
>
> (Unknown)

We are agency pros based out of New York (Kristin) and London (Shalon). (Hi there!) We met in a public relations (PR) agency, led several global teams together at two different agencies for multiple clients, and pretty much have seen it all.

We value service, both to clients and to teams. In working together, clients always came first. However, as managers, we were constantly finding opportunities to teach after years of growing in our own careers. We believe that the uplifting guidance of a generous mentor was much more beneficial to us than floundering on our own, which we did plenty of early on. Agency work is greatly team based, so it's important to understand not only PR but the secrets that make successful agencies tick. Unfortunately, many of those secrets are revealed only after years of experience – until now.

In this book, we draw on our own personal experiences rising in our careers and as agency leaders to explain what it takes to thrive as an individual, as a team member, and as a client partner in a PR agency.

2 Who Is This Book For?

> If I was down to my last dollar, I would spend it on public relations.
> (Bill Gates)

If you have fewer than 10 years of experience in a public relations (PR) agency, this book provides practical advice and shortcuts to success. Why learn all the lessons the hard way, right? This book is also a must-read for anyone entertaining the idea of going into the industry from college or another career, so you know what you're in for.

PR is all about the team, and the work the team produces is not always visible, but its impact can change the world. While personal acclaim is in short supply in PR, you'll get a solid adrenaline fix since a busy PR agency always delivers an exhilarating work environment. Every day there is an opportunity to work on new challenges spanning multiple and often complex issues. PR is a fast-paced industry, and from the moment you wake up until the moment your head hits the pillow, it's go time.

Adrenaline aside, PR agencies are complex and often peculiar organizations to navigate. Although your job satisfaction can be greatly shaped by co-workers and client relationships, the office environment, and the impact of your projects, you're not going to get far on that ladder until you truly understand what it takes to be indispensable. Recognizing that billable hours are currency, flawless execution is expected, and new business is a mandatory extracurricular activity is only scratching the surface of what you need to know. If you're interested in a successful career in PR, why waste time figuring it out yourself, when you can just turn the page?

3 What's in It for You?

> Either write something worth reading or do something worth writing.
> (Benjamin Franklin)

There are great books on public relations (PR) theory, and industry rocking case studies. There are also hundreds of books that focus on management consulting, principles of outstanding client service, and leadership philosophy. Much of what's out there is instructive, best practice material that you should learn and know. However, until now there has been no book that synthesizes theory and practical advice of all of the subjects above to demystify the unique environment, culture, and skills necessary to be successful in a PR agency.

PR can be an enthralling or a frustrating career experience depending on how you juggle and perceive the many facets required to be a success. In an agency, patience, diplomacy, endurance, and imagination underpin successful campaign ideas and relationships with clients and colleagues. The difference between those who succeed in an agency environment and those who throw in the towel is often simply one of understanding the business structure, which is unique to PR agencies.

This book is going to help demystify why things are the way they are in PR agencies. If you understand the system from the get-go, then you can work it to your advantage to succeed faster. It wasn't just serendipity that we, the authors, had leadership positions in our twenties while leading major accounts and big teams – we figured out how to make ourselves indispensable.

In addition to practical advice about the agency system, you've also signed up for a dose of real talk and personal brand coaching. The intersection between what you say, what you do, and how you're perceived will dictate whether you're revered as indispensable in a PR agency or any other job.

No matter your title or billing rate, if you ever think what you're being asked to do is "busywork" or below you, then you already have the wrong attitude to succeed. Every task is on someone's plate for a reason, and who gets what generally comes down to aptitude, competence, years of expertise, enthusiasm, capacity, and which mix of billing rates is going to turn a profit. This book is going to teach you how to build a brand and maneuver the system so you get to do more of what you want, sooner, and become a go-to for clients and colleagues in the process.

Part II

Agency Basics

Whether you are new to a PR agency or think you know it all, this part will help deepen your understanding of agency structures and dynamics.

PR agencies seem straightforward. Teams of people win new business pitches to bring in client work that ranges from awareness campaigns to brand communications to corporate reputation management and everything in between. Account teams are then formed to work for clients who are billed on a retainer basis or hourly for work completed. At the most basic level, that's all true. However, if you look closer, agencies are structured to serve many masters – both inside and outside – resulting in a matrixed organization that can complicate client service, best practices, team dynamics, staffing, and finances.

In this part, we will:

- unpack agency structures, roles, and how teams are formed;
- clarify new business processes;
- present a comprehensive overview of finance in a PR agency;
- explain writing essentials that underpin exemplary client service, including guidance to avoid 'rookie' mistakes (and it's not just newbies making these mistakes!).

4 Architecture of Agency Life

> Learn the rules like a pro, so you can break them like an artist.
>
> (Pablo Picasso)

Agency Ecosystem

What agency is right for you? To get you closer to that answer, you really have to understand how agencies are organized, and how that organization may influence your experience. In the era of globalization, you may be surprised to learn that both privately held and publicly traded agencies are often brands owned by global marketing communications holding companies. DJE Holdings, a private company, owns global agency Edelman, Zeno Group, and others, for example. It's even more common – almost ubiquitous – for public companies to follow this model (see Table 4.1). Publicly traded WPP plc (NASDAQ and London: WPP), OmnicomGroup (NYSE: OMC), Publicis Groupe (EPA: PUB), Interpublic Group (NYSE: IPG), or Havas Group (EPA: HAV) all have multiple agency brands under their umbrellas.

The decision to work for a privately held or publicly traded agency will make little difference in your day-to-day work. However, publicly traded companies have stricter processes for financial planning, tracking, and reporting, given legal accountability requirements. This may affect hiring, promotions, and compensation. The effects of stricter financial processes are felt most acutely at the senior levels of the agency, where financial management, oversight, and ultimate accountability rests.

Agency Structure: Hierarchy versus Flat

Most public relations (PR) agencies are structured similarly whether they subscribe to a hierarchy of job titles or prefer a "flat" organization, where there are no titles but a basic hierarchy still exists. A flat structure is often thought to instill a greater sense of ownership and merit-based opportunity unfettered by corporate role expectations. Although this may all sound very liberating, let's not delude ourselves. Employees and clients alike use hourly billing rates,

Table 4.1 Marketing Communication Holding Company Heavyweights

Holding Company	WPP plc	Omnicom Group	Publicis Groupe	Interpublic (IPG)	Havas Group
HQ Listing	London, England NASDAQ: WPP LSE: WPP	New York, USA NYSE: OMC	Paris, France EPA: PUB	New York, USA NYSE: IPG	Puteaux, France EPA: HAV
Annual revenue	$15 billion+	$15 billion+	$9 billion+	$7 billion+	$2 billion+
Global footprint	200,000 employees in 112 countries	70,000+ employees in about 100 countries	80,000+ employees in 100+ countries	50,000+ employees in 100+ countries	20,000 employees in 100+ countries
Leading PR agency brands	• Burson Cohn & Wolfe • Finsbury • Hill & Knowlton • Ogilvy Public Relations	• Cone Communications • Fleishman-Hillard • g+ Europe • Ketchum • Porter Novell	• Manning Selvage Lee • Publicis Worldwide • Starcom	• Carmichael Lynch Relate • ID Media • Golin • Weber Shandwick	• Havas Worldwide • Abernathy MacGregor Group • AMO

Note: Most recent figures available at the time the book was written which escalate with experience, as proxies for titles. See Figure 4.1 for an example of roles in a flat organization and titled hierarchy. It is more common for agencies to use a titled hierarchy structure.

Flat Organization	Titled Hierarchy
Director level	Managing director (MD) Senior vice president (SVP)/senior director Vice president (VP)/director
Manager level	Managing supervisor (MS) Senior account supervisor (SAS) Account supervisor (AS)
Junior level	Senior account executive (SAE) Account executive (AE) Assistant account executive (AAE) Account coordinator

Billing Rate

Figure 4.1 Agency Structure: Flat Organization (left); Titled Hierarchy (right)

Regardless of title, people will do great work, take responsibility for their deliverables, and seek opportunities to stretch their skills if they feel supported. For example, people with a couple of years of experience – junior staffers – are often asked to conduct media outreach around a press release to secure articles about a client's recent news announcement or product launch. Junior staff must be taught what reporters want and how to pitch effectively, but they may be too shy or proud to ask for support when it's not proactively offered. As you may already know, it's really difficult to persuade overwhelmed reporters to write about your news even if you have existing relationships with them or are skilled at pitching, so imagine how scary it is if you don't know what you're doing! No matter your place in a flat structure or hierarchy, it will be challenging to be successful if you're not asking for support when you need it or offering enough of it when results are at stake.

Both titled hierarchies and flat organizations have benefits and pitfalls. Titled hierarchies may feel confining, but they provide clarity in roles, power dynamics, and progression. Flat organizations can make you feel like the sky's the limit; however, that may be daunting if your trajectory is unclear. Power dynamics and promotions can be mysterious in flat structures, and junior staff may be left with unrealistic expectations of what their daily workload should entail. The lack of clarity can often lead to amorphous roles at all levels, where new responsibilities are dressed up as skill-stretching opportunities instead of being treated properly as a promotion.

Here's the thing – each agency type has its pros and cons so you just need to pick the structure that fits best with how you work and with what you value (see Table 4.2).

Table 4.2 Apples and Oranges: Hierarchy versus Flat Agency Structures

	Titled Hierarchy	*Flat Organization*
Role definition	• **Pro:** You know exactly what is expected of your role, which is often summarized in a job description. • **Con:** Role is so clearly defined that it can stifle learning and growth opportunities.	• **Pro:** Roles are flexible and it may be easier to capitalize on opportunities to grow skills. • **Con:** Roles are flexible so you could be redeployed if there is a business need.
Day-to-day work	• **Pro:** The expectation of what you need to deliver in each rung of the hierarchy is clear and correlated to level of experience/expertise. • **Con:** If you can complete work "above" your title, you still may not be given the opportunity to do so.	• **Pro:** If you're wildly talented, you will be given as much work and opportunities as you can handle. • **Con:** Junior staff may perceive they are "above," or too advanced for some types of work and senior staff may be expected to do work that is not a good use of their talent and experience.
Progression	• **Pro:** It's clear what the next step is and what is required to get there. • **Con:** Ladder-climbing may create cookie-cutter employees focused on checking boxes to get to the next title versus encouraging creativity and curiosity.	• **Pro:** Structure supports people to pursue strengths and interests. • **Con:** The path to a promotion is unclear because a promotion may or may not be based on a billing rate increase or a change in responsibilities.
Reporting lines	• **Pro:** The pecking order is clear. You know who your boss is and who you are managing. • **Con:** Rigidity of the structure may not allow for hybrid roles or exploring new opportunities without a formal role change.	• **Pro:** Tend to be matrixed so you gain exposure to a lot of different people you can learn from and mentor. • **Con:** You may technically report to one person, but are expected to answer to many, which can lead to misunderstood or conflicting reporting expectations.

Account Team Structure

For the newbies, let's take a minute to review how teams are structured. Whether you're working in a hierarchy or a flat organization, or whether your PR agency brand is large or small, public or private, all agencies organize in teams with varied levels of experience and expertise. Each team is dedicated to one client. It's possible – and very likely – that you will work for multiple clients, on multiple teams, and will need to become adept at juggling.

The team structure in an agency, regardless of whether it's a hierarchy or flat organization, generally includes a regional leader at the top, who serves as an accessible senior strategic counsel and participates in strategic planning meetings and activities alongside someone in an account director role. Account directors lead the account teams' execution of the strategy, control work quality, and serve as the first escalation point for a client. Account managers who own discrete projects are the daily points of contact for a client, and move most deliverables to completion. The junior staff are guided by account managers to complete the work agreed upon with the client according to their level of experience and/or ability. The core team is then supported by specialists such as media, digital, creative, research, and others who integrate with the core account team as needed.

References

Havas Group. "Documents & Reports: 2016 Annual Report." *Havas Group*, 2016, www.havasgroup.com/finance/documents-reports/.

Havas Group. "Documents & Reports: Fact Sheet." *Havas Group*, 2016, www.havasgroup.com/finance/documents-reports/. Accessed 22 May 2018.

Interpublic Group (IPG). "About: Overview: More about IPG." *IPG*, www.interpublic.com/about/overview. Accessed 22 May 2018.

Interpublic Group (IPG). "Investor Relations: Financial Reports: 2017 Annual Report." *IPG*, 4 Nov. 2018, http://investors.interpublic.com/phoenix.zhtml?c=87867&p=irol-reportsannual. Accessed 22 May 2018.

OmnicomGroup. "About: Overview: Global Leader in Marketing Communications." *OmnicomGroup*, www.omnicomgroup.com/about/. Accessed 22 May 2018.

OmnicomGroup. "Agencies: Get to Know Our Agencies." *OmnicomPublicRelationsGroup*, www.omnicomprgroup.com/agencies/. Accessed 22 May 2018.

OmnicomGroup. *Annual Report 2015*. *OmnicomGroup*, 2015, http://s2.q4cdn.com/400719266/files/doc_financials/annual_reports/2015/Omnicom-Group-Inc-2015-Annual-Report-to-Shareholders.pdf. Accessed 22 May 2018.

Publicis Groupe. "Publicis Groupe: 2017 Financial Results." *Publicis Groupe*, 2 Aug. 2018, www.publicisgroupe.com/en/news/press-releases/publicis-groupe-2017-annual-results. Accessed 22 May 2018.

WPP plc. "About: At a Glance." *WPP*, www.wpp.com/wpp/about/wppataglance/. Accessed 22 May 2018.

WPP plc. "Contacts: Companies." *WPP*, www.wpp.com/wpp/companies/. Accessed 22 May 2018.

WPP plc. "Investors: Share Price: Basic Share Information." *WPP*, www.wpp.com/wpp/investor/shareprice/. Accessed 22 May 2018.

Industry Insight

MIKE KUCZKOWSKI

Chief executive officer (CEO), Orangefiery
San Francisco, California, USA

Agency life... the phrase has such an appealing ring to it. Big clients, important issues, brilliant team, a wealth of talent to tap into. But what's it really like?

When I arrived at Edelman in 2002, the Corporate & Public Affairs group in New York was a 34-person department. There were lots of great individual players who had expertise in things like public affairs, crisis, corporate social responsibility, tech, financial communications, and media. Our office didn't have scale yet around these specialties. In a group that size, everyone pitched in on everything. Being new to "Big Agency" life, the variety was a dream come true. They put me on an issues management project involving mining reclamation bonds. And tech clients. And financial clients. And education clients. The experience I got from this was gold: I helped build a website (so novel in 2003!), ran a media center, managed crises and led a piece of business for a pharmaceutical industry client that laid the foundation for the business I run today.

Times have certainly changed. Agencies increased their specialization around practices (consumer, technology, public affairs, corporate) and then around their clients. In recent years, they have pioneered entirely new organizational models, with roles like planners, creatives, and community managers that never existed before. Some of this has been about growth. Some of it has been about the demand for greater expertise from clients. And some has been about new capabilities around emergent communications channels and trends.

Take a close look at the model, though, and you can see its seams. Think about it, what do technology, healthcare, consumer, corporate, and digital have in common? Two are industries, one is an audience, one is a corporate function, and one is – well, you tell me, it seems the definition of digital is constantly changing. When everything gets specialized, how do you have an impact in an area like communications, which spans such breadth of a client's needs?

When I think about my professional journey, I was truly blessed to have the opportunity to be a part of such a broad range of assignments. It shaped my perspective on communications, the importance of stakeholder insights, and the value of narratives and engagement in achieving business goals. And it led me to start a small agency, where everyone is expected to pitch in on everything. What's right for you? The best answer for me comes down to fit and opportunities. When you're early on in your career, the thing you should most look for is experience that can help you grow as a professional. Big, small, flat, hierarchical. Find a group of people you like and respect, dive in, and see where the currents take you. The one thing I can guarantee you about agency structure is, it's bound to change.

After starting his career in journalism and politics, Mike has spent the last 20 years in agency life. He spent 12 years in various roles at Edelman, including general manager, global client relationship and president of Edelman Consulting. In 2014, he started Orangefiery, an agency focused on healthcare communications.

5 The Life Cycle of Business

> The only place success comes before work is in the dictionary.
> (Vince Lombardi)

Business development or "biz dev" is the lifeblood of all agencies and everyone takes part at various points in the process throughout their career. In fact, biz dev is one of the best opportunities to showcase your strategic, creative, and organizational skills to get noticed by leaders within the agency as a rising star.

Like many aspects of agency life, biz dev is stimulating, challenging, and always on a short timeline. Since agencies are generally not staffed sufficiently to cover peak client workflow and pitching for new clients, it's likely that at some point you will be expected to help outside of your billable hours – before or after standard working hours and sometimes even on weekends. That said, new business can be a lot of fun! Imagine – a prospective client comes to your agency with a request for information (RFI) or a request for proposal (RFP) that outlines an unmet business objective . . . and you get to help figure out how the client can achieve it.

Most agencies have a dedicated biz dev lead or small team responsible for securing opportunities and driving processes, such as responding to RFIs and RFPs, in addition to supporting account teams with expanding their current projects within a client, otherwise known as "organic growth."

Requests for Information

It is common for larger companies with a procurement function to ask potential vendors (like public relations (PR) agencies) to submit a detailed form (often an excel spreadsheet) about its services (eg areas of expertise in both skills and subject matter, client references) and operations (eg size, global footprint, financials, corporate structure) for future consideration. A member of a PR agency's biz dev team is normally in charge of responding to RFIs since they will have all the information at hand from prior submissions.

Many prospective clients also want to hear right from the source about how great your services and team are by chatting with an agency's current clients. If you work on one of the agency's larger accounts, or just in general are known for having really happy clients, biz dev is likely to reach out to you to submit a client contact to serve as a reference. Obviously, you have to ask your clients if they are open to being a reference. Ambushing clients with a call from a prospective client or procurement is one of the quickest ways to damage your relationship, even if they are over the moon with your team and quality of service. Generally, clients are open to providing references as long as they are confident their day-to-day account team will not be compromised if the agency took on the new piece of business.

You may be wondering how companies looking for a PR agency figure out who to consider in the first place. There are quite a few ways for an agency to get on procurement's radar, including the following.

- *Personal connections/introductions*

    You don't have to be on the agency's biz dev team to help originate prospective client leads. Most biz dev teams are eager for you to introduce them to potential new business contacts. To that end, remember you're sticking your neck out for the company, so make sure they're going to do right by your contact. Also, you should be financially rewarded for bringing business through the door, so make sure you have that discussion with your bosses and leadership before brokering any introductions. In our early days, this was a rookie oversight we both learned in our eagerness to be "helpful" and a "team player." Many agencies have a referral bonus in place.

- *Cold-calling/procurement roadshows*

    A member of the biz dev team may call a company's procurement team unsolicited to offer to submit an RFI or for an agency executive to deliver a short presentation of the company's credentials and capabilities (affectionately known by most as "creds" or "capes"). Usually, the biz dev team will try to make the most of their executive's time by booking a tour of procurement meetings called a "roadshow."

- *Industry awards*

    Winning *PRWeek*'s agency of the year or other industry accolades is a sure way to gain positive attention, reinforce credibility, and help raise the agency's profile for when prospective new clients are searching on Google.

- *Word of mouth*

    If a PR agency is doing great work, word will spread and procurement will invite an RFI response.

If a company looking for a PR agency partner doesn't have a procurement function, it is unlikely that your agency will receive an RFI and will be asked directly for an RFP instead.

Requests for Proposal

Once procurement has reviewed a PR agency's RFI and added it to a list of preferred vendors, the next step in the new business process is for the agency to receive a formal RFP. Most companies will not ask more than three or four PR agencies to submit an RFP response, and many already have favorite agencies that will be selected to compete. It can be challenging for an agency to get an invitation to submit an RFP response. If a company doesn't have a procurement function, they don't have the benefit of having a pool of vetted PR agencies to choose from, so they often invite a larger group of agencies to submit proposals.

RFPs are normally a 10-page document delivered as a Adobe PDF file and usually include:

- background on the company;
- background on the brand, product or function the PR agency will potentially service;
- timeline and deadlines;
- RFP contact;
- rules for engagement, such as submitting a signed confidentiality agreement, destroying documents used in the RFP process once the agency partner is appointed, etc;
- the main assignment, which is generally to write a communications plan for a strategic challenge (eg product launch in a saturated market, awareness campaign for a target audience, etc) and to contextualize the solution within the agency's expertise (eg case study evidence to show your agency has done this successfully so many times that you can do it in your sleep). Often the main assignment will require a response within a specified number of pages or slides;
- additional information requested, which may include a creds and capes deck, proposed account team structure, biographies of proposed account team members, budget estimate for the cost to execute the main assignment, and the PR agency's rate card detailing each team member's cost per hour, assuming the agency bills on an hourly rate structure (most common).

RFP deadlines and formatting requests should be taken seriously. It takes a tremendous amount of work for an agency team to put together a considered

RFP response, and the last thing anyone wants is to be disqualified because a submission was five minutes late, a deck was a slide too long, or a document wasn't named properly. Let's be honest, if you're reading this book, then you're probably intrinsically motivated and possibly a perfectionist, and you don't need something small to spoil all of your hard work.

Following an RFP submission, an agency is normally notified if it's been cut or if it's been "shortlisted." Getting cut means just what it sounds like and getting shortlisted means that the PR agency has made it through the first round of consideration and is asked to present its RFP response main assignment in person to a group of company representatives. Generally, the agency adapts its RFP submission deck to be more visually dynamic and prepares to be asked tough questions following the presentation. This presentation is known as "the pitch" and induces anxiety and stage fright in even the most seasoned PR veterans. However, these nasty symptoms can easily be eliminated with the cure-all – preparation – and its sister remedy, critical thinking.

PR agency team members who participate in the pitch vary, but normally include a managing director (MD) and senior members of the proposed account team. On the company's side, the pitch is usually attended by the procurement contact, potential client, potential client's boss, and various people from marketing, corporate communications, and/or the brand team.

You're probably starting to get a sense that an RFP submission and subsequent pitch is a massive undertaking. Also, you're offering up a lot of brilliant ideas that, ultimately, a prospective client might not hire you to bring to life (but could still use!). For this reason, it's critical that an agency's leadership is selective about which RFPs the company participates in. What's worth the investment? Leaders who try to capitalize on every RFP opportunity may find themselves in a bind with current clients. The new business process is resource-intensive and both physically and emotionally demanding for the team members involved in the preparation, which can lead to employee burn-out or rushed, poor quality work. Although the biz dev team is often working to different metrics than account teams, it is essential to remember that the first rule of new business is that existing clients come first. And, like *Fight Club* (1999), this is also the second and third rule. The fourth rule is that nobody talks about how many caffeinated beverages were consumed in the making of the RFP response and everyone pretends not to notice if you're wearing the same clothes as the day before.

So, your fearless leader has strategically elected to participate in an RFP and the biz dev lead is starting to mobilize. Table 5.1 shows a best practice of how the process *should* go, with the knowledge that RFP deadlines are generally tight; the average timeline only provides about 10 business days to prepare a response.

Once an RFP response has been submitted, it normally takes a of couple weeks to find out if your agency has been shortlisted. If selected to pitch,

Table 5.1 RFP Response Best Practice

Timing	Activities	Detail	Questions for Consideration
Day 1	Request for proposal (RFP) participation decision	(Biz dev lead) Communication to the RFP contact that the agency will or will not participate, and develops a timeline to prepare the RFP response. (Managing Director (MD) & biz dev lead) Identifies and engages an account team to work on the RFP response and proposal for the potential client.	MD • Is this an area/company one of our new business targets or one of our agency should be working for? • Do we have the resources needed to produce a killer pitch while maintaining high-quality work for existing clients? • Are my account teams exhausted from back-to-back pitches? • Do I have the right resources to put forward an account team if we win the pitch?

Days 2–3	Research	(Biz dev lead)
		
		• Research is assigned to junior members of the biz dev and/or proposed account team, generally broken into:
		   ◦ traditional media audit;
		   ◦ social listening;
		   ◦ summarizing analyst reports;
		   ◦ expert interviews;
		   ◦ competitive mapping;
		   ◦ influencer mapping.
		• Research is compiled into a pack with a summary that outlines the company/brand/product's current situation in the marketplace. A list of questions is compiled for the agency Q&A call with the RFP contact and submitted in advance. The call itself may transpire during any of the stages of RFP response development so any new insights need to be pulled through.
			(Biz dev lead)
			
			• Who are the target audiences this company/brand/product needs to reach?
			• What perceptions does the target audience currently hold about the company/brand/product?
			• How does the media and/or analysts cover the company?
			• What motivates target audience behavior?
			• Which channels or people influence the target audiences?
			• Where does this company fit within its competitive landscape? (ie a leader or a copycat offering)

Day 4	Strategy development	(Biz dev lead)
• Convenes a strategy meeting with the MD and senior counsel on the proposed account team. Prior to the meeting, participants need to have read the research pack
• Any additional research identified during the strategic brainstorm is completed and circulated
• Following the meeting and final research, either biz dev or a senior counsel converts the output of the meeting into a strategic framework and circulates for review and consensus

(Biz dev lead)
• A force-field brainstorm can often be quite helpful during strategy development meetings:
  ○ Write the current situation from the research pack on the left side of the white board
  ○ Write the ideal situation based on goals/vision for success from the RFP on the right side
  ○ Identify any challenges or barriers between the current and ideal situations
  ○ Brainstorm strategies to overcome each challenge or barrier and which audiences need to be influenced to execute the strategy |
| Day 5 | Tactical ideation | (Biz dev lead)
• Convenes a meeting with the MD, proposed account team, specialists (eg digital, creative, etc) and any other talented people he or she thinks may contribute
• A few tips:
  ○ ground the meeting in the strategy and don't leave the door open for commentary on the strategy–focus on the tactics;
  ○ have the meeting in the morning when everyone is fresh;
  ○ only schedule the meeting for 1.5–2 hours;
  ○ structured ideation exercises are more effective than a traditional "vomit-ideas-on-a-flip-chart" brainstorm;
  ○ limit the meeting to eight people or less. | (Biz dev lead & senior counsel(s))
  ○ Who does this tactic target?
  ○ Why will this tactic be effective?
  ○ Is this tactic realistic? (eg cost, logistics, etc)
  ○ Is this tactic aligned with the RFP expectations? (eg are the potential clients expecting a "big idea," or a budget launch?)
  ○ How do we measure success? |

(continued)

Table 5.1 (continued)

Timing	Activities	Detail	Questions for Consideration
Day 6	Writing	(Biz dev lead & senior counsel(s)) • Draft the upfront of the deck based on the research, followed by the strategic and tactical frameworks • Biz dev lead, account team and specialists write tactical and measurement slides • Biz dev junior team compiles creds and capes if needed and liaises with in-house or external graphic designers to bring the RFP response deck to life and give it a polished look	(Biz dev lead & senior counsel(s)) • Does the upfront tee up strategy and tactics? • Does the proposal flow? • Does this proposal answer all the questions in the RFP assignment? • Is the deck within the RFP response parameters?
Days 7–8	Design & budget	(Account manager & senior counsel(s)) • While the deck is being designed, the account manager on the proposed team can compile a budget for the Senior Counsel(s)' review. • Deck design is reviewed and budget submitted.	(Account manager & senior counsel(s)) • Are the budget line items consistent? • Were out of pocket expenses considered? • Is contingency budget included? • Does the budget fit within the parameters of the RFP or potential client's expectations? If you don't know what the expectation is – make sure to ask! If they say the sky's the limit, then make sure the budget is modular so when reality sets in clients can easily prioritize what they want to pay for

Day 9	Review & amends	(Biz dev lead & senior counsel(s)) • Review the deck and make any needed amends before conducting a final walk-through of the deck and budget with the MD	(MD) • Does the upfront tee up strategy and tactics? • Does the proposal flow? • Does this proposal answer all the questions in the RFP assignment? • Are all the tactics within budget? • Is the deck within the RFP response parameters?
Day 10	Proofing & submission	(Biz dev lead) • Assigns junior staff to proof all documents being submitted as part of the response before the deadline	(Biz dev lead) • Do all the documents meet formatting, length and naming requirements outlined in the RFP?

an agency is normally given two weeks to a month to prepare, which is a combination of presentation and Q&A. Typically, a pitch is scheduled for a time slot of about 90 minutes – one hour for presentation and 30 minutes for questions.

An agency is generally allowed to adapt the RFP response slides for presentation by making them more visually interesting and to go in-depth into any aspect of the proposal that requires additional explanation. The agency will usually send three to five people to pitch: agency MD, senior strategic counsel, day-to-day team leader, junior team member, and a relevant specialist. It's critical that everyone who attends has a meaningful speaking role and that only people who are going to work on the business are in attendance (aside from the MD). Clients do not like the "bait and switch," when agencies send their "A team" in to pitch and once the contract is signed, they swap out the team.

How to Kill It in a Pitch

- PREPARE, PREPARE, PREPARE! Nothing is going to help you win more than knowing the material like the back of your hand and being able to communicate clearly, confidently and, most importantly, succinctly.

- Spend time with your pitch team. Clients can feel if the team is going to work well together based on the dynamic. Clients want to work with a team that respects and supports each other. The better the team dynamic is, the more potential clients will want to work with you.

- Bite your tongue if someone else has already elaborated on a point. If a potential client asks a question and someone on the team answers and then someone else on the team elaborated, but missed a point, let it go. It doesn't look good when teams pile on top of each other to make a point.

- Be gracious to everyone for everything, from the admin to procurement. And always take the high road about agency competitors and the potential client's competition. It makes you look unprofessional and insecure to criticize the competition.

- Demonstrate judgment. Don't disclose anything about another client that could be confidential or isn't already in the public domain. If you spill the beans about another client, then the potential client may think you would have the same transgression with their information.

- Lastly, be authentic. It helps cultivate trust, credibility and, essentially, a rapport. People want to work with people who are genuine, fun, and pleasant.

Organic Growth

If you're authentic and do great work, your client probably can't get enough of you. Great client service and relationships usually lead to new projects with and without an RFP. Obviously, it's ideal to win projects without an RFP process because it's more profitable – there's a limited upfront resource investment in putting together a small proposal for a project with a client you already know. The RFP response, however, requires a lot of agency resources for a client that may or may not hire you . . . and there is no compensation for pitching.

The best way to grow accounts is to do great work and to offer solutions to problems and challenges that the clients mention to you, or that you identify as something that could meaningfully improve the client's business. Pushing services and products onto your clients simply to get more budget is idle work at best and unethical in some worst-case circumstances. Also, it generally doesn't work and could weaken your relationship. Recommendations should always be in the best interest of your client. If your client has mentioned how challenging it is to get a consumer perspective on a topic, and your agency specializes in social listening – it's a natural fit to offer to help.

How to Win Business from Existing Clients

- *Do great work on time and on budget*

    Your client will want to give you more projects/work and/or word will get around the company and your client's colleagues will approach you to work on their projects.

- *Offer solutions to challenges*

    Be a cold sell and offer to put together formal or informal proposals/quotes – be flexible to provide whatever information is helpful to your client to make a decision. Don't badger your clients with follow-ups – let them come to you when they're ready.

- *Invest in the relationship*

    We're not talking about bonding through a great night out (though there can be a place for that, too!), but rather offering to provide a specific, finite service, gratis. For example, if an existing client isn't digitally savvy, but wants to leverage Twitter, offer to have your digital specialist provide a Twitter boot camp lunch 'n' learn for your client's department. This could be beneficial on two additional fronts. First, clients want to work with subject-matter experts, so positioning your PR agency as an expert is advantageous. Second, it's an opportunity to expose the agency to new potential clients within the company.

- ***Decline projects that won't be successes***

    Don't take on projects that could potentially tarnish your sterling reputation within a client. Politely decline the project if:
    - it isn't your expertise;
    - you won't be able to deliver on time/budget;
    - you don't have enough resources to deliver to the highest standard;
    - it won't be profitable for the agency;
    - it is with a difficult stakeholder that could affect team morale or the agency's reputation within the client company.

Ultimately, new business is rooted in common sense and authenticity, which makes many parts of the process accessible to all levels of the agency organization.

Reference

Fight Club. Directed by David Fincher, Twentieth Century Fox, 1999.

Industry Insight

THEA LINSCOTT

Vice president of business development, MSL
New York, USA

Business development is often perceived as a mysterious world of endless possibilities and solutions. I would say that in my role, I simply build people to be the best version of themselves, powered by research and data to create brilliant strategies to solve pressing problems for clients, and convince them of it, too.

However, business development isn't just about a new pitch or the best ideas. Whether you're looking to win a new client or hoping to impress your current client, you have to tune into the client's personal business goals and key performance indicators. Tap into how you can really drive their business. What makes change for the client? What do they value? How does the data influence the strategy? Where should you throw tradition out the window and really get creative? It's exciting to consider the possibilities when given the challenge of solving a problem. Having the answers to these questions and more is what makes a stronger relationship and better outcomes for your clients.

Understanding that is critical, and it's something that should always be happening, regardless of any specific opportunity. There are always other agencies, opinions, news, cultural shifts, internal forces, and more, changing the needs of your client, so constantly thinking about how to add value and advance your client's business is fundamental. It also helps grow your business and relationships.

(continued)

(continued)

I personally love the biz dev and the process because you get a challenge and then, with research, both qualitative and quantitative, you can apply smart thinking toward a common goal. There are so many details involved in all of that and it can be emotional and charged. Crazy, insane, awesome, terrifying, and wonderful all come to mind when thinking about new business – especially if there are multiple pitches happening at once. Yet, a high-pressure environment yields great thinking and great outputs that solve our clients' greatest challenges and can even change the world. There are not many other roles you can say that about.

Thea is a seasoned communications expert with a focus on business development and strategic growth at MSL, one of the world's largest PR and integrated communications firms.

6 Money Honey

> The price of greatness is responsibility.
>
> (Winston Churchill)

Ask a classroom of public relations (PR) majors if they're "numbers people" and you're guaranteed to hear groans. It's unusual for communication experts early in their career – and perhaps even in mid-career – to identify as "numbers people." Those who work in PR often don't have confidence that they are strong in math or finance. But we need to squash that thinking here and now.

The reality is – like it or not – that if you're going to be successful in any business, including PR and client services, then you need to be good with numbers. Why? Money, honey.

Financial management is a central part of running a successful client account team – your business – at a PR agency. When you're managing a PR account on behalf of a client, you're managing a "piece of business." This business not only has to be well-managed, but you also need to understand how the success of the client's business fits into the overall success of your agency. There are many financial responsibilities and considerations, and anyone in an agency or corporate communication leadership role will agree that the most successful people are great communicators and numbers people.

The first part of understanding "the numbers" is understanding what governs them. So, not only do you need to know some finance, but you need to know some legal stuff. Much of this will be stipulated in the contract established between an agency and a client. It will dictate things like billing rates, invoicing responsibilities, payment terms, and penalties for late payments. There will also be important things in the contract that affect budget, such as when it's okay to charge a client for a cab while working late, or whether it's permissible to book a business-class flight over an economy-class flight if traveling on behalf of the client (get that neck pillow ready because it's almost always economy!). All of these things are important and ultimately affect the budget. If you're managing a client's account, it's your responsibility to know and understand what's within the contract.

One thing to note – sometimes the contract takes months to develop. In larger PR agencies, the legal team usually works with the client's legal team to negotiate the terms. While you have to know what's in the master services agreement, you normally aren't part of the back and forth of contract negotiations. However, you should never start working with a client until a formal work agreement is in place. What to do if you don't have a contract ready, but the client is pushing to begin work? Have your legal advisor draw up a letter-of-agreement (LOA), sometimes referred to as a memorandum-of-agreement (MOA). Like a contract, it's a written list of goods or services to be provided at agreed-to prices, in terms and time. It's less detailed than a contract but will ensure you some protection for getting paid for the work you do if there were ever a disagreement.

Contract (and LOA/MOA) details aside, at a PR agency, day-to-day financial management of a client's account generally includes three core components:

- Project scope
- Billing
- Invoicing

Let's look at each of these more closely.

Establishing a Project Scope

In any client relationship, first and foremost, it's important to define the project/work that is going to be done. Often, the definition or agreement for the project/work to be done is called the "scope of work," "SOW," or "project scope." In some agencies, it's simply called the "project agreement." For now, we'll use the term "SOW." Just as the name varies, the SOW contents can vary as well. Despite the variance, in best practice we can assure you that it always includes seven elements:

- Objective
- Strategy
- Tactics
- Deliverables
- Metrics
- Timeline
- Budget

Solid PR counsel is grounded in strategy, so it's critical to restate the client's objective and outline the strategy and tactics – the "how" – in the SOW. Equally important is establishing, in writing, what deliverables the client can expect.

Deliverables simply means the "what" that you are going to produce for the client, such as a timeline, a press release, or a launch plan. Keep in mind that deliverables influence the budget. A portfolio of photographs and videos of the client's product, for example, can be costly, especially if you have to bring in an external photographer or videographer to produce and edit these assets.

Metrics need to be established in the SOW so that there is agreement on what success looks like. Metrics should be tied to how outcomes of the effort support the objective that is also outlined in the SOW. It's all related. And, while it might be tempting to overlook metrics, which often include data and analysis and therefore seem less "fun" than other PR activities, they're essential to measuring and agreeing what success looks like. For example, you might develop a social media content strategy that increases a client's following by 500 percent, but if the client wanted to increase engagement with a specific segment of their target audience and wasn't fussed with follower quantity, then you will have a lot of disappointment to manage. Your idea of success and the client's understanding of "success" must align.

The timeline is important because it sets expectations for how quick, or how slow, it will take to make things happen. Timelines also affect the budget, since projects that take 10 days will be less expensive than projects that take 10 months, assuming hourly fee billing.

Once all the components of the project are outlined, a budget for the work can be established. There's a little bit more to creating a budget, and we'll reveal that to you in Chapter 7. For now, just know that it's the final component of the SOW.

The SOW is presented to the client for clarification, negotiation, and/or approval. If a client has questions about the SOW, that's a good thing! It means that the client is thinking critically about what you're about to do on his or her behalf, and this gives you the opportunity to ensure there's no misunderstandings about what will be done, why it's being done, how it's being done, when and for what amount. Ideally, work should not start until an approval has been established and there is confirmation that the budget is ready to bill against; however, most relationships begin with an abbreviated SOW inside a LOA.

Billing the Client

It's typical that PR agencies will bill in one of two ways. The first, though less common, is a flat project rate billing. The second, which is more common, is an hourly fee billing. Let's review each billing option:

- *Flat project rate billing*

    A flat project rate is just what it sounds like – a flat cost for the project outlined in the SOW. The flat project rate may also be called a "flat rate," "flat fee," or "retainer." However, take note that this is not the same "retainer" billing model that you'd see in other industries, for example, law.

    In the flat project rate billing model, the agency provides the final cost to the client versus a budget estimate based on potential hours worked. If the client agrees, the cost will be the amount charged to the client unless the scope or timeline changes. The key is to renegotiate the change order before doing the work. Clients never like to be surprised by additional costs.

    Flat project rate billing may include out-of-pocket (OOP) expenses, but don't have to. OOPs are anything external that you can generally charge on a credit card (eg newswire fees, venue rental, catering, airfare, etc).

- *Hourly fee billing*

    Hourly fee billing models are the most popular billing method in PR agencies. Fee, in this case, is only "people" time, and clients are only charged for actual hours worked. The fee, or people time, is one component of the budget estimate and the OOP is the other. OOP is never included in the fee, which again is only people time.

    Recall that in the PR agency structure, there are many roles from junior staff all the way to global executive leadership. On the account team, each role has an hourly fee – a dollar amount – associated with the title or level of expertise. Thus, junior staff time costs the client less than senior management staff time.

    In the hourly fee billing model, the budget estimate includes what an agency thinks the project in the SOW may cost, based on how many hours team members at each level are estimated to spend on the project. This estimate is presented to the client for approval. Nevertheless, unlike in a flat project rate billing model, where the budget set is the money you are actually guaranteed to get, a budget based on hourly fees is only a "reserve" of money that your client will pay after you've already worked the hours. The agency can bill up to that budget amount, but never wants to go over.

Invoicing

A PR agency submits an invoice to the client based on the contract and budget agreements. This is how you get money for the work, and again why it's important for you to be a diligent "numbers person."

Table 6.1 Billing Models' Pros and Cons

Pros of Hourly Fee Billing	Cons of Hourly Fee Billing
• **Constant revenue stream:** Invoices are generally submitted monthly. • **Less likely to "over service":** An hour worked = an hour paid (however, this is only if everyone on the team spends the agreed number of hours on each task and enters their time accurately). • **Helps managers keep staff at healthy production levels:** Every .25 of an hour is coded, so it's easier to see who is overworked and who has capacity to do more work.	• **More administration:** Every .25 of an hour is coded, so yes, there is even a code for coding time! • **Susceptible to "nickel & dime" discussions:** A client may hesitate to pick up the phone and call you if they think it will cost an extra 15 minutes in fee. • **Decisions may be made based on the budget versus the strategy.** • **More difficult to financially forecast:** We can estimate how many hours will be worked each month, but it's not guaranteed because it's common for deliverables to be brought forward or delayed which impacts the workflow (know that despite this dynamic, account directors are still required to forecast how much revenue they're going to bring in each month for the entire year).

Pros of Flat Project Rate Billing	Cons of Flat Project Rate Billing
• **Clients see the "big picture":** The focus is on getting the project as a package. • **Less administrative management:** No time tracking unless it's needed to determine profitability, no activity reports are needed to justify hours, and there's fewer invoices to keep track of. • **Scope is narrowly defined:** Because there is a risk to "over service," all work promised to the client should be tightly scoped and narrowly defined. The advantage is that the client will know exactly what will be delivered and there is greater clarity on what's included and what isn't. • **Get paid what you're worth:** An admirer once asked Picasso to draw her something on a napkin in a café and she offered to pay whatever he thought it was worth. He said that will be $10,000. She said, but you just drew it in 5 minutes and he replied, it took me 40 years and 5 minutes. Senior communication professionals often do things that take only a few minutes, but the impact to the client's business can be huge. Why should clients only pay for the few minutes it took to make the call or get the advice? With a flat fee, clients can be charged the value of the service versus the time it takes to provide it.	• **Tendency to "over service":** Because time may not be tracked, people may take longer than needed to complete tasks. • **Poorly written scopes can erode profits:** Often what seems like a straightforward project may suddenly have all sorts of time-consuming details crawl out of the woodwork that clients will expect to be covered if the scope is not incredibly tight and specific. • **Potentially lower liquidity:** Since invoices are sent in lump sums (example: beginning and end of project), there is more time between working and getting paid. Keep in mind that operating expenses still keep rolling in.

With flat project rate billing, the client will pay a specified amount at a specified time. An example would be to pay one-third of the budget at the start of work; one-third midway through; and the final one-third at completion. Regardless of what's in the contract, the payment terms should be reiterated and clearly agreed upon in the SOW, which outlines the budget.

With an hourly fee billing model, payment terms will be outlined with greater specificity in the contract. With this billing model, the agency usually invoices clients monthly for actual hours worked. For example, if an account executive's billing rate was US$150 and an account manager's billing rate was $250, and they each worked 10 hours for the month, the client would be invoiced for $4,000 ($1,500 + $2,500) out of the full budget. Monthly invoices are submitted to the client, and typically are accompanied by an "activity report." An activity report is simply a written outline of work performed to justify the accumulation of hours.

Pros and Cons of the Billing Models

Like anything, there are pros and cons to each billing model. Neither is better than the other per se, but they each offer advantages and disadvantages depending on the number of clients an agency services, the size or complexity of the agency team needed to complete the scope, and the size of the client's budget. Table 6.1 outlines the pros and cons of each model.

Industry Insight

CHEN LIANG

Consultant, Ruder Finn Asia
Hong Kong, China

If you have been asked to estimate a budget – congratulations, you are a step closer to becoming a team leader. At the end of the day, PR people also have to be "numbers people." Of course, only a handful of industry professionals study finance or accounting in university, so numbers often incite more fear than excitement in most. But trust me, a solid knowledge of numbers will be the key to unlocking unparalleled confidence and trust from your clients. More importantly, it may not actually be as difficult to understand as you think.

PR budgets can be divided into several categories: fee, cost, and OOP (don't be intimidated by any of the terms). Since costs and OOPs can only be determined on a case-by-case basis, I will focus on fees here. Always think about the two "Ts" – Team and Time.

Team: How many people should be put on the team to serve this client/complete this project (one assistant account executive (AAE), one senior account executive (SAE), one consultant, and one director)? What are their roles and responsibilities? When it comes to descriptions of tasks and the scope of work, you can never be too detailed. Don't hesitate when listing a breakdown of the number of press releases, editors to pitch, etc.

Time: How much time do you expect each team member to allocate to each task? Hours per week? Days per month? Put everything into a Microsoft Excel spreadsheet. This will clearly show the totals. Ta da, easy, right?

(continued)

(continued)

The last piece of advice I can offer is always to give yourself some buffer when creating a budget. This comes from a series of hard lessons where I was trying to make my client happy by setting a lower budget – and it came back to haunt me. One of my global retail clients wanted to host a cross-border livestream event from the New York flagship store for audiences in China. I calculated everything (or at least I thought I did), except the equipment needed to support the signal transmission, which was different in the USA and China. Ultimately, I went over budget due to this difference. Another memorable case was when, during an evening movie premier, the backdrop was missing the logos of our major sponsors! We had no choice but to print the logos and stick them on one by one. We also had celebrities asking for more security, challenges with the lighting equipment, a shortage of badges; the list could go on and on . . . and it all required extra budget.

It might be hard at first to ask the client for a large chunk of money, but if you're honest about what you need it for upfront, it will save you money in the end. The client will be happier to see that you ended up saving them some money, instead of having to ask for more along the way. And, amazingly, you will always find that the "leftovers" will eventually be allocated somewhere else anyway.

Chen is currently a consultant at Ruder Finn Asia in Hong Kong and previously worked for a broad range of organizations in New York, including PSE&G, Monique Péan, and the United Nations. Chen has a master's degree in public relations and corporate communication from New York University.

7 Budget Basics

> A budget is telling your money where to go instead of wondering where it went.
>
> (Dave Ramsey)

Surprise! You're also a part-time accountant who understands law. Who knew public relations (PR) professionals were so versatile? This chapter builds off the "Money Honey" (Chapter 6) fundamentals to apply billable hour concepts to building budgets and making staffing decisions.

Remember in Chapter 4 where we introduced the idea of agency structure? As we mentioned then, most agencies operate with a hierarchy. Take another look at Figure 4.1 to jog your memory (see page 11).

Got it? Okay, put a pin in that, because we're building a puzzle together. Now we want you to recall what we talked about in Chapter 6 regarding how agencies invoice. There is a flat project rate billing model and an hourly fee-based model; most PR agencies use the latter.

So, to really expand on budgeting in this chapter, we're going to look at how to create a budget, assuming our agency uses a staff hierarchy and hourly fee billing model. The following is what you could expect to see at the largest, leading PR agencies.

Scenario: You are a Vice President at a PR agency, "Agency X," and you and your team just successfully pitched the prospective client, "Boombastic Candy," an international retailer of candy and other novelty food products. In the pitch, you gave your biggest and best ideas – the sun, the moon, and the stars – and let them know that the big picture might be a $2–4 million budget depending on what they include.

Fast forward two weeks and guess what? They loved your ideas, they loved you and your team, and now you're hired! The "big ideas" in the pitch now have to be refined into a specific and measurable scope of work and budget. How do you do that? Well, it's a bit complicated, but ultimately, it's not that hard.

38 *Agency Basics*

1. **Create your SOW**

    What is the objective(s) that you want to commit to as a team? Which strategies, tactics, and deliverables will be included to achieve success? You will have to hold back on building the budget until you know the "staff mix" (who is on your team and at what level) and the billing rates.

2. **Build your team**

    Some of the team members will already have been selected during the pitch process, but you may need to bring others onto the team as well. Hold that thought because we're going to dive into how to build a successful team in Chapter 16.

3. **Consult your contract**

    To see what the billable hourly rates are for each of your team members. If you've just constructed a core team, each person on that team will have a "billable" rate attached to their title. Recall, the more experience someone has, the higher their billing rate will be. Check out Figure 7.1 for an example.

Core Team

Penny Plumbaum, J.D.
President & Senior Partner,
Issues & Crisis Strategist

George Baker
Senior Consultant,
Media Strategist

Sophia Woodstock
Managing Director &
Partner, Public
Affairs Lead

Joy Nguyen
Vice President,
Day-to-Day Lead

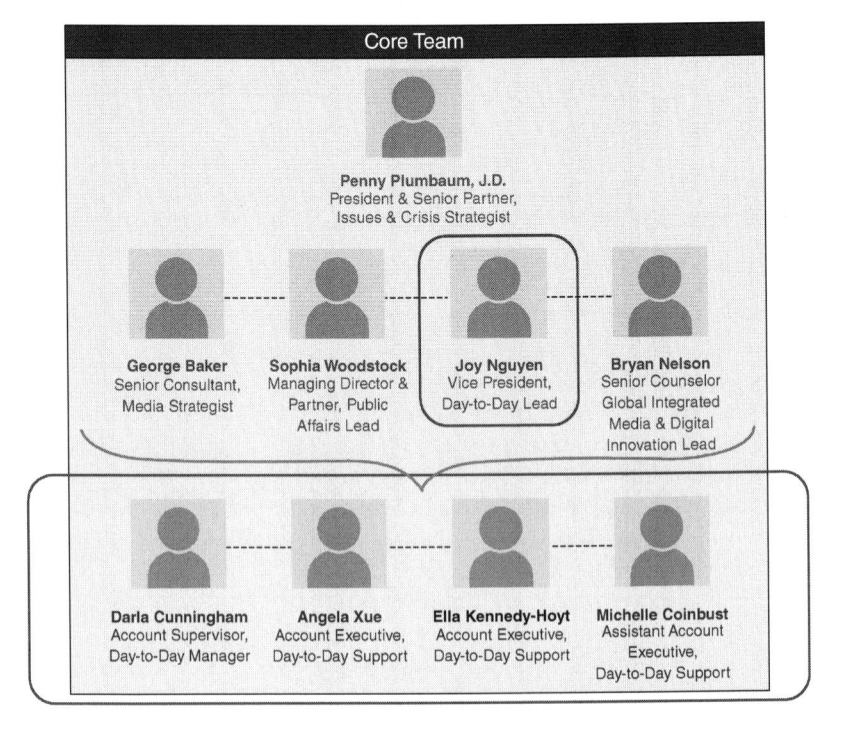

Bryan Nelson
Senior Counselor
Global Integrated
Media & Digital
Innovation Lead

Darla Cunningham
Account Supervisor,
Day-to-Day Manager

Angela Xue
Account Executive,
Day-to-Day Support

Ella Kennedy-Hoyt
Account Executive,
Day-to-Day Support

Michelle Coinbust
Assistant Account
Executive,
Day-to-Day Support

Figure 7.1 Agency X's Core Team for Boombastic Candy

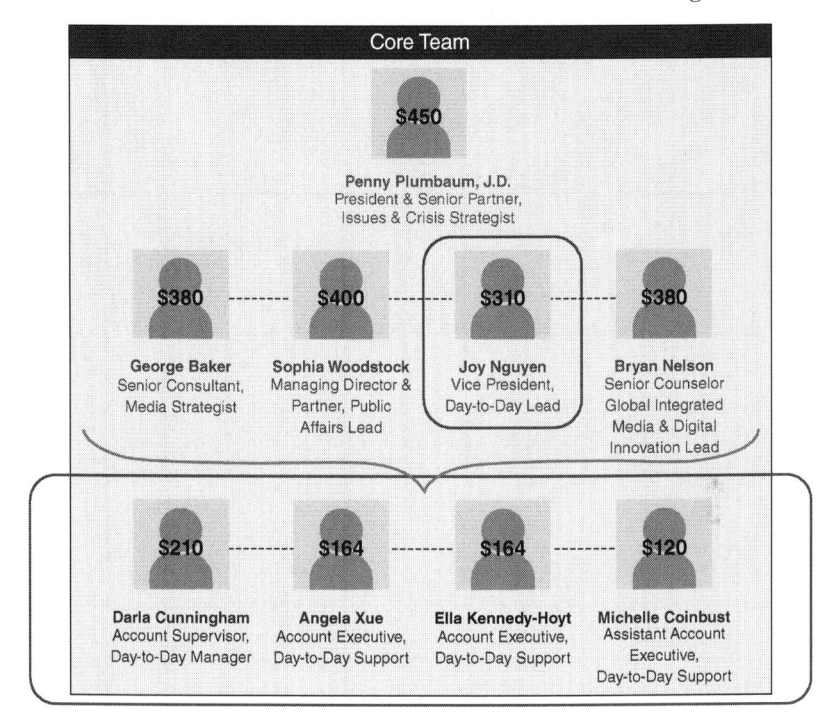

Figure 7.2 Agency X Hourly Billing Rates for Boombastic Candy Account

In this scenario, Joy will be the day-to-day lead of the account team. The day-to-day team who will support her includes Darla, Angela, Ella, and Michelle. Each of these team members will have different responsibilities depending on their experience and their capacity, or availability, and billing rate. In Figure 7.2, you can see that when Agency X consulted their contract with Boombastic Candy, they were able to see the billing rates for every title.

Going back to our SOW, let's pretend that one of the tactics for Boombastic Candy is to create a press release. Seems simple, right? The reality is that there are many more pieces to that puzzle, including:

- weekly client calls;
- reading background materials;
- finding references for industry statistics;
- developing messages around the announcement;
- multiple release drafts depending on how many layers of review it has to undergo within the client's organization;

- creating a reference pack – the back-up showing exactly where all the information in the release came from;
- identifying who will be the spokesperson and securing quote approval (and if the spokesperson is an external expert, you'll need the approval of the communications department of their organization as well);
- paying for the OOP cost to put the release on the news wire, which is typically between $300 and $5,000 depending on the service used, word count, and distribution choices, such as geography and topical circuits (eg food reporters in the USA and Europe).

When you're looking at everyone on the team, tracking every .25 hours, it suddenly becomes very important to be precise about how much time each person is spending on each activity. Imagine, a 15-minute team meeting alone would cost the client's budget $242. A one-hour team meeting each week – budgeted for a month – becomes nearly $4,000 (see Table 7.1 below). Note that in addition to meeting attendance, it would be reasonable to estimate that an account executive might spend up to 30 minutes establishing the agenda or preparing for the meeting and up to 30 minutes capturing notes and action items following the meeting. This additional activity could add another hour each week to the estimate.

Our tip to you? Become a Microsoft Excel pro. It's essential for projecting and forecasting – which is basically predicting how much time it will take to do something and how much it will cost the client's budget as a result. When building the budget, you have to account for every single thing because once the budget is set you are committed to it. Why? Going over budget means that you need to ask your client for more money, which shows poor planning on your part as an agency leader. If the client agrees that more money is needed, then they need to go back to their bosses and get the money. It's uncomfortable for everyone and ideally the budget is right the first time.

Table 7.1 Team Meeting Budget Calculation

Team Member	Weekly Client Meeting	Total Hrs	Billing Rate	Total Billing
President	0	0	$ 460.00	$ -
Managing Director	0	0	$ 420.00	$ -
Vice President	4	4	$ 310.00	$ 1,240.00
Senior Account Supervisor	0	0	$ 260.00	$ -
Account Supervisor	4	4	$ 210.00	$ 840.00
Senior Account Executive	0	0	$ 186.00	$ -
Account Executive	8	8	$ 164.00	$ 1,312.00
Assistant Account Executive	4	4	$ 120.00	$ 480.00
Total Hrs	20	20	Grand Total Fee	$ 3,872.00

That said, don't over-project and underspend. If you have significant budget left over – because remember, you can only invoice for time you actually work – then you also have a problem. Why? Clients have to work hard internally to secure their budgets. There's only so much money to go around in an organization, and a client trusts you to project the correct estimate. If a client works hard to secure $1 million this year, and only $800K is spent, then $200K that could have been used in other places within the client's company is sitting unused. This means that the following year, when the client goes back for $1 million for your team's PR budget, it's more likely you'll only get $800K and will have to scale back on your PR plan as a result. Bottom line: get the budget right and manage it well.

When the budget is approved, a billing code system is set up so that as the PR account manager, you can see with granularity who is working each aspect of the project to manage the budget accurately. We have learned that it's important to sub-divide the budget, but it's better to have larger buckets that address chunks of the projects, so you have flexibility if one activity takes less time and another takes more. If you have a billing code for every activity, then you often need to get written permission from the client that you're allowed to reallocate funds between billing codes/budget lines or your agency's accounting department won't let you. Make sure to check time weekly as a lot can happen in a month, and you may find yourself overspent if you're not on top of how the budget is being worked.

Let's pretend you have a $200K budget over four months. In one scenario, it may be reasonable to split the money evenly, which means you and your team can spend $50K per month for four months. But $50K is a lot to manage, so perhaps the team breaks that up further to represent the work for the month. For example:

June – $50K projection

- Team meetings – $5K
- Content development – $20K
- Media relations – $25K

The team members will be recording every 15 minutes of their day to a billing code that corresponds with each activity bucket. For example, Joy, the Vice President of the Boombastic Candy team, might spend her Monday allocated to the following.

- 1 hour: team meeting (billing code 12345-0)
- 2.5 hours: materials review (billing code 12345-2)
- 1.5 hours: campaign brainstorm (billing code 72727-3)

- .5 hours: reviewing graphics proofs (billing code 88888-0)
- 3.5 hours: client meetings/correspondence (billing code 12345-1)

In Joy's nine-hour day, she is billing her time to five different codes. Each code corresponds to a different budget. At junior levels, agency team members are simply told to allocate their time. At the more senior levels, however, you will actually be the one projecting and forecasting how much time each person on the team spends on each activity. Surprised? The reality is that at the most senior levels of a PR agency, about half of the job is time, people, and budget management. Running an account is truly the equivalent of running a small business.

One final note on budgeting. In some cases, work on a project will begin before a budget is finalized, but after the contract or LOA/MOA is in place. That work is called "work in progress," or WIP. It should be tracked and included in the final budget.

It seems strange to start work before a budget is in place, but there are many scenarios where this could happen. For example, let's say your client would like to consider having a celebrity spokesperson join the campaign. Your team would do a ton of research to see which celebrities would be interested, and who would be a fit for your client. You'd put recommendations together and share them with your client. All of this would eat up hours, which equals fee (in an hourly fee billing model). The time spent on this research would be considered WIP, assuming your contract states that you can bill the client for research and proposal development, and it would be "moved" to be a part of the final budget that's created for the celebrity spokesperson. Therefore, if your ultimate celebrity campaign is estimated to be $100K, and you have already spent $15K in research hours (WIP), the total budget you'd propose to the client would be $115K.

Industry Insight

BANKS WILLIS

Senior vice president, Spectrum Communications
Washington, DC, USA

First the bad news: as a PR agency professional you will have to work with numbers and spreadsheets. This may seem counterintuitive; PR professionals are good with words, not numbers, right?! Plus, if you're anything like me you *might* have made your first school career C in third-grade math. Here's the good news: client budgets are much more than just a number – how we manage our client's budget actually represents the value of our services. The minute I shifted my mindset, I was almost immediately more empowered, productive, accountable – and valuable. So, how can you start facilitating your own budget enlightenment?

Time is money. Consequently, whatever your role is on an account, whether you're a formally staffed member or simply pinch-hitting for a colleague, proactively ask questions to ensure that you are doing your part to spend the client's money wisely. Ask the account manager "How much budget do we have?" "How much time is reasonable for me to spend on this project?" and "What code should I bill my time to?" Don't allow yourself to live in the dark, or take the easy way out; the sooner you learn the better.

I knew someone who knew someone who got an email from a client inquiring about a $6K invoice they received. There was no traditional activity report attached to justify the team's activities. The client ultimately asked for an activity report from the head of finance at the agency, but the team could only account for about $5K of work.

(continued)

(continued)

It's not that they were falsifying hours, but they weren't tracking time, and the project manager wasn't proactively monitoring the budget. This scenario happens when nobody is minding the shop, not the project lead, not her number two, and not even a pinch-hitter. Though a refund was issued to the client, their trust, which is priceless, was affected.

Everyone at every level needs to care about a client's budget. If things are not appropriate, they shouldn't be billed to the client, and this includes onboarding – you should never learn on the client's dime. Clients hire you for expertise, so the billing should reflect that. It's all about being a good budget steward and valuable player to the client.

Banks is a healthcare corporate communications and public affairs leader with 20 years of experience across corporate in-house, consulting, and government environments. She currently leads public affairs for healthcare-focused communications firm Spectrum Communications.

8   Staffing

> Delegating work works, provided the one delegating works, too.
> (Robert Half)

Staffing Teams

Assembling multiple account teams is sometimes referred to as the "staff mix." Teams are assembled by many criteria, including specific skills and strengths that address the client's needs, such as sector experience; the experience level of each team member which if working in "billable hours" corresponds to the billing rate; the client's budget; and relationships, including preference for team members with existing positive relationships with the client or the client's company.

Staffing teams seems straightforward. However, staffing challenges can arise when assembling a team for a new client for a variety of reasons, including:

- people put forward in the account team structure do not have capacity for new projects;
- the agency does not have the right staff mix to do the work but agrees to take on the business anyway;
- the agency does not have enough resources to complete the work promised and needs to hire to fill gaps;
- client fees are not high enough to sustain the proposed account team structure.

One challenge of the public relations (PR) agency business model is that until additional revenue is secured through the confirmation of new business (ie new budget!), additional staff cannot be hired. This means that almost every time a PR agency pitches for a new account, they will not have enough staff or the right staff mix of expertise to immediately do the work if they win the business. During a pitch, clients want to meet the team they will actually be working with. Nonetheless, due to the agency hiring process this is often a paradox because the team that attends the pitch is usually already fully occupied with existing accounts.

Trying to overcome the paradox often has a domino effect down the account team structure that can make it challenging to deliver superior counsel, high-quality work, and quick response times.

- The regional leader ends up going to the pitch to secure the business, and to a meeting or two a year to keep the business; otherwise, they are inaccessible unless there is a crisis or the client complains.
- An account director is required to overstep the boundary of their role due to the scarcity of the regional leader, or because they do not have the right staff mix, and/or clients fall in love with them and request them to be more involved than needed. This can result in account directors being stretched too thin and/or working extra hours to stay on timeline and maintain team work quality.
- Account managers are often promoted to the role too quickly and do not have the skills or experience to perform the role as it was intended, which leads to the account director quality controlling work they otherwise would not.
- Junior staff are eager to do the senior staff's work and push for client exposure and more complex assignments while turning their noses up at their current workload and learning opportunities as "beneath" them. Turnover can be quite high at this level because they think they'll get more advanced work if they change agencies. Spoiler alert – generally not! You need to crawl before you can walk.
- Specialists are not always integrated at the most opportune time or are stretched too thin to provide attention to a new project.

How do you take a potentially challenging staffing situation and create a successful account team? Read Table 8.1 for a taste of what it takes to build a team, but we'll go into greater detail in Chapter 16.

Staffing by the Numbers

We may have mentioned this before – Microsoft Excel is your new best friend. In PR agencies that bill on an hourly fee model, time is money. You have to do the math to make sure you have the right amount of people's time to do the work within budget, without giving work away for free, also known as the dirty word, "overservicing." It's kind of like the old American game show, *The Price Is Right*. You have to get to the max of your budget, without going over. Overworking a client's budget due to inappropriate staffing eats into your company's profit (and ultimately affects everyone's annual compensation). Overservicing due to staffing errors can

Table 8.1 Quick Guide to Thoughtful Staffing

Questions to Contemplate	Considerations
1. What is the team's goal and values?	• Is this a one-off project or ongoing account? • What does the client view as success? • What should be valued most to achieve the goal? (eg creativity, dedication, collaboration, etc)
2. Which skills are the most critical for the team to achieve its goal?	• What is the client's disposition and working style? • What composes the majority of the work? (eg strategy development, issues management, digital/social, media relations, content development, measurement, graphic design, etc)
3. Who in the agency has the required skills, expertise, and level of experience?	• Identify the ideal team and back-up options if your first choice doesn't have capacity.
4. Are there enough client fees to support the billing rates of these people to deliver the work?	• Develop a billing power worksheet to guesstimate. Don't know what a billing power worksheet is? See the "Annual Billing Power" section.
5. Do these people have enough capacity to be on the team?	• What's the capacity plan look like? Don't know what a capacity plan is? See the "Monthly Capacity Planning" section. • Check with people's managers to make sure they are available, are not being reserved for other projects, and that this project is aligned with their professional development goals.
6. If there is not enough capacity, is there any flexibility in the current workload to make capacity?	• Can you trade resources with other managers to pull the ideal team together?
7. Would a reallocation be beneficial to the agency or would hiring be better?	• Will taking someone off their current account/project impact the client relationship? Will the change make that person unhappy or be a match made in heaven?
8. What added value does each available team member bring?	• Are there secondary skills in the identified core team that can help fill staffing gaps?
9. What limitations does each person have and can they be offset by another team member?	• Have you chosen people with complementary skill sets and personalities? • Will the team members get along? Are there any underlying politics that will affect productivity?
10. Is each team member's personal values aligned with the team's values?	• Based on your knowledge and experience with a person, will they value what the team needs to value to be successful and achieve the goal?

really undercut an otherwise healthy client relationship, especially if you are getting pressure from above to ask the client to cover the overage.

The following sections describe two tools to help staff an account appropriately.

Annual Billing Power

This spreadsheet provides an educated estimate to see if the team assembled will be able to deliver the client fees within the specified time frame based on how much time each person can commit and their billing rate.

Let's break down how we calculated Jane's billing power from the sample spreadsheet in Figure 8.1:

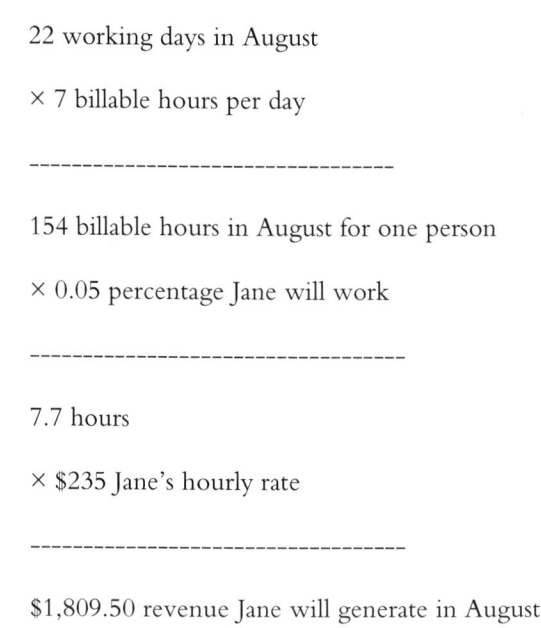

22 working days in August

× 7 billable hours per day

----

154 billable hours in August for one person

× 0.05 percentage Jane will work

7.7 hours

× $235 Jane's hourly rate

$1,809.50 revenue Jane will generate in August

The total power calculated (Figure 8.1) should match the client's fee budget. If the number is lower than the client's budget, then you may need to add staff or secure additional percentages of current team members. If the number is too high, then you're overstaffed and will have to reduce people's time commitments or remove them from the account. Both types of staffing changes should consider the scope of the account or project to ensure that added team members will have enough work to do suitable to their level of expertise, or that the team can still deliver without the person who was removed or had their capacity reduced.

If a team is assembled to work a project, you only need to plan for a few months, but most people reading this book will need to plan for a year or the rest of the calendar year from when they win the business as most

Sample Account A

Team Member	Title/Role	Rate	Allocation	Aug	Sept	Oct	Nov	Dec	Total
Work days per mo				22	22	21	22	20	
Hours per mo*				154	154	147	154	140	
				Monthly Billing Power					
Jane	Managing Director *Senior strategic counsel*	$ 235	5%	$ 1,810	$ 1,810	$ 1,727	$ 1,810	$ 1,645	$ 8,801
David	Account Director *Senior client lead*	$ 185	25%	$ 7,123	$ 7,123	$ 6,799	$ 7,123	$ 6,475	$ 34,641
Tom	Senior Account Manager *Day-to-day client lead*	$ 155	50%	$ 11,935	$ 11,935	$ 11,393	$ 11,935	$ 10,850	$ 58,048
Samantha	Account Manager *Project manager*	$ 140	50%	$ 10,780	$ 10,780	$ 10,290	$ 10,780	$ 9,800	$ 52,430
Mike	Account Manager *Media specialist*	$ 140	20%	$ 4,312	$ 4,312	$ 4,116	$ 4,312	$ 3,920	$ 20,972
Jessica	Senior Account Executive *Content development*	$ 125	65%	$ 12,513	$ 12,513	$ 11,944	$ 12,513	$ 11,375	$ 60,856
John	Account Executive *Content development*	$ 100	75%	$ 11,550	$ 11,550	$ 11,025	$ 11,550	$ 10,500	$ 56,175
Mary	Assistant Account Executive *Graphic design*	$ 75	30%	$ 3,465	$ 3,465	$ 3,308	$ 3,465	$ 3,150	$ 16,853
Total power				$ 63,487	$ 63,487	$ 60,601	$ 63,487	$ 57,715	**$ 308,775**

Figure 8.1 Annual Billing Power Worksheet
*Based on working 7 billable hours per day

account budget cycles are annual. It's also best practice to conduct this exercise when planning a team for the following year, especially if the client's budget has changed or the team has evolved/turned over.

Monthly Capacity Planning

Since accounts and projects don't run at a consistent pace every month, it's unlikely that a team's billing will match the billing power. Work will ebb and flow with deliverable deadlines moved forward and decisions delayed. Thus, a "capacity plan," often called a "staffing plan" or "staff allocation plan," helps reveal over/understaffing by month across all the accounts in an agency. The plan is based on each account director's forecast of how much of each client's budget he or she expects to work that month depending on the team's scope of work, action list, and client calls/correspondence.

The capacity plan is updated monthly, starting with people's percentages from the billing power and then adjusted up or down based on the amount of client fee budget the account director expects to work. Most agencies have a monthly capacity planning meeting to discuss the directors' input to the spreadsheet. Generally, during these meetings, people's time is reluctantly given to other teams if their account is overstaffed, and often directors who find themselves understaffed need to come up with a creative solution to get enough hours to deliver the work. This may entail: working long hours; borrowing spare time across the agency for low-level work; engaging a freelancer; or even borrowing a person from a sister agency or other business unit within a holding company.

This is not a perfect process. Most capacity planning meetings are long and it's common for agencies to struggle to address staffing issues during work peaks. Competent freelancers are hard to find, especially on short notice, so there is value to capacity planning quarterly rather than monthly to provide advance visibility of potential staffing challenges.

Industry Insight

MEREDITH TOPALANCHIK

Senior vice president, G&S Business Communications
Member of the Public Relations Society of America (PRSA), PR Council, and Penn State Bellisario College of Communications Alumni Society Board
New York, USA

The most important thing I've learned about staffing in my nearly 20 years in PR agencies is empathy. Empathy for our team members, empathy for our clients, empathy for our leadership, and empathy for our financial management team.

I have the benefit of being client-facing and overseeing our talent, recruiting, professional development, and cultural efforts for the entire agency. Because PR is more art than science, often agencies focus solely on the data and numbers associated with staffing. Clearly this is important for budgets and profitability, but if you ignore the human dimension, you will ultimately falter.

Here are the top five things that I've learned about staffing in a PR agency:

1. Having a dedicated person or small team looking closely at the data and also staying in tune with the health and well-being of your staff will lead to success.
2. If you execute staffing with a team mindset, the agency and clients win.
3. Remember clients get attached to their team members, but don't be afraid to switch it up to give people more opportunities and room to grow; it will help them thrive at all levels of career.
4. Staff members are constantly learning new skills and mastering others. Give them that latitude to stretch and grow – it will pay off in the long run.

(continued)

(continued)

5. Clients are changing strategy and asking for more. The media is rapidly changing and consolidating. If we don't adapt to these variables and consider the tangible *and* intangible it can make staffing very challenging!

Whether you are early on in your career or in charge of staffing the team, it's important to remember: Happy staff = happy clients = a happy (and profitable) PR agency.

With nearly two decades of PR agency experience, Meredith combines a passion for media and client relations with a strong, strategic, creative voice. In her role as senior vice president, she provides counsel to international blue-chip clients and also leads the agency's talent and culture group, which allocates staff, executes recruiting and onboarding, creates professional development opportunities and wellness programs.

9 Ethical Conduct

You're never wrong to do the right thing.

(Mark Twain)

As this book is about how to be successful in a public relations (PR) agency, we'd be remiss not to touch on ethics. On your climb up the proverbial ladder of agency life, at every level there will be many decision crossroads. At the mention of crossroads, you might envision a fork in the road, where one clear path splits into a road to the right and a road to the left. This idea of one road splitting into two is how many people think of decisions. Should I go left or go right? Do I say "yes" or "no"? Is something good or bad?

Unfortunately, in real life, the crossroads aren't always clearly defined. Sometimes, it's difficult to know what is right, what is wrong, and what falls in between. Much of it falls in between.

This is where ethics come into play. Ethics are your code of conduct. Professional ethical principles in PR guide how you should act in decision crossroads, but there is never black and white clarity. Ethics in action are "values" lived – think of values as "the show of the tell" and "the walk of the talk." A company can speak about putting the clients first, declining new business that represents a conflict of interest, and committing to professional development, but if doesn't actually do these things, then it is not living its values or operating within its ethical principles.

An important point of clarification: ethics are a code of conduct provided by an external source like your workplace or a religion. Whereas morals refer to personal principles of right and wrong. It's good to have your morals intact, simply so you know what you stand for and what you don't.

Ethics, values, morals – oh my! "Why does this really matter?" you might ask. It matters because your career in PR is based on your reputation, and your reputation is your greatest asset. In order to nurture that asset, you have to know who you are and what you stand for – as an individual and as a professional. As you grow in your career, your reputation will follow you and, in order for you to build it, you need to be consistently working in the interests of your client and your company – and also yourself. And, if we haven't said it before, we'll say it again: hundreds of people have the technical skills. What will set you apart is *you*. Your reputation is like a résumé for all that can't be captured on paper, such as trust, responsibility, and partnership.

Don't just take our word for it. The Public Relations Society of America (PRSA), the professional organization guiding the PR industry, has a comprehensive statement of professional values which demonstrate ethics lived. They include:

Advocacy

We serve the public interest by acting as responsible advocates for those we represent. We provide a voice in the marketplace of ideas, facts, and viewpoints to aid informed public debate.

Honesty

We adhere to the highest standards of accuracy and truth in advancing the interests of those we represent and in communicating with the public.

Expertise

We acquire and responsibly use specialized knowledge and experience. We advance the profession through continued professional development, research, and education. We build mutual understanding, credibility, and relationships among a wide array of institutions and audiences.

Independence

We provide objective counsel to those we represent. We are accountable for our actions.

Loyalty

We are faithful to those we represent, while honoring our obligation to serve the public interest.

Fairness

We deal fairly with clients, employers, competitors, peers, vendors, the media, and the general public. We respect all opinions and support the right of free expression.

(PRSA)

These values are not only about preserving your reputation. Adhering to professional ethics elevates the entire industry. Consider for a moment that the origins of PR began with "the engineering of consent," as was famously coined by the father of modern-day PR, Edward Bernays (113). (More on

Bernays in Chapter 15!) The idea that PR professionals engineer consent or manipulate has led to offensive stereotypes such as "spin-doctors," "hacks," or "fixers," none of which encompasses the commitment to relationship building that defines PR today. To counter that, we must consistently act in ways that defy negative stereotypes, and support the meaningful role PR plays in building relationships and understanding between organizations and their employees, customers, government, and the media.

Sometimes, following professional ethical guidelines isn't easy. For example, if you morally disagree with a client's business, but you agree to represent that client, you have an ethical duty to do your best work for that client even if it advances something you morally object to. In the event that your morals preclude you from doing your best work for the client, it's your ethical obligation to resign from the account. However, that's easier said than done – especially if it puts you out of work.

In addition to supporting both your and the industry's reputation, adhering to professional ethical guidelines will keep you out of trouble. Capturing client hours, for example, is an area that is always under great scrutiny. We get it – tracking every 15 minutes of your day to a billing code is the last thing you want to do at the end of a 12-hour day. Yet fudging 15 minutes here, 30 minutes there, or even an hour or more equals fraud (and will derail the client's budget). Fudging hours is not only unethical and against industry best practice, but it's also illegal. We're serious – top ex-PR executives have gone to jail for this.

The same goes for disclosing non-public information. You might be in the know on a soon-to-be public announcement that will change the world – and affect the stock market. Guess what? If you spill the beans on an announcement early to select friends or family, and they make trades based on that information, you've just been implicated in insider trading. That's jail time too.

We don't want to scare you with the slammer. Hopefully, you'll be compelled to uphold ethical guidelines because it's the right thing to do for your clients, company, teams, industry – and you! But there is a lot to consider as you embark on your agency career, and certainly who you are and what you stand for is all part of the package.

References

Bernays, Edward L. "The Engineering of Consent." *The Annals of the American Academy of Political and Social Science*, 1947, pp. 113–120.

Public Relations Society of America, Inc. (PRSA). "Code of Ethics." *Public Relations Society of America*, 2018, www.prsa.org/ethics/code-of-ethics/.

Industry Insight

MICHAEL ESTEVEZ

Managing director, public affairs and crisis communications, Burson Cohn & Wolfe
New York, USA

Resolving ethical dilemmas is a matter of values. In my experience, such dilemmas occur when an organization lacks authentic values or its leadership adheres to them inconsistently. As a communications counselor, part of your role is to help clients live up to their values in difficult times – and that fundamentally begins with ensuring you live up to your own.

Once, I was in discussions with a potential hospitality client that would have represented a sizable contract for my firm. They were involved in a sexual harassment lawsuit in which their former head of housekeeping, who was bilingual, was accused of harassing members of the housekeeping staff. The housekeeping staff was primarily undocumented female immigrants who only spoke Spanish. When I pressed the prospective client about what reforms they implemented to avoid a future recurrence, they effectively responded, "None. We just want this to go away." I immediately ended the discussion.

In my 20-plus-year career, I've helped clients manage scores of issues from international patent litigation to handling noise complaints from nearby residents. It's been exceedingly rare that a client has ever faced a true high-stakes dilemma in which there were "multiple right answers." In the few cases where that's occurred, my advice has always been simple: choose the course of action that most closely aligns with your values, commit to it, explain your reasons why to your key stakeholders, and remain steadfast in your decision against all opposition. It's advice I've also chosen to live by, and it's served me well throughout all kinds of professional crisis situations.

> Michael is a managing director in Burson Cohn & Wolfe's Public Affairs and Crisis practice based in New York. He advises clients on crisis and litigation communications, issues management, and cyber-security risk communications.

10 Writing Essentials

> Words are, of course, the most powerful drug used by mankind.
> (Rudyard Kipling)

As expected, writing underpins every facet of public relations (PR) and is another skill integral to success in a PR agency (and as far as we're concerned, life – but of course we are writing a book "for fun" so we would say that!).

Okay, so you won writing awards in high school and aced your lit classes in college *or* you've been in a professional job for years . . . so you don't need writing advice, right? You probably want to read the rest of this chapter unless you:

- can recite *The Elements of Style* (Strunk and White) by heart;
- have never made a spelling error in an email, text, WhatsApp, Facebook message, etc;
- have never sent an email or text to the wrong recipient;
- have persuaded someone you've never met in person to let you manage tens of thousands of dollars of their budget through a single email.

Now that we have your attention, we can assure you that you're not alone. The reality is that all of us have made some writing mistakes somewhere along the way, and as the famous writer and editor William Zinsser said, "rewriting is the essence of writing." So, take note of our top 10 tips to avoid "rookie" mistakes.

1. **Be humble**
   It doesn't matter how much of a perfectionist you are or how many years of experience you have, you're going to make many mistakes because you're human. Thus, you need to rely on your team to have your back and catch those errors before they are submitted to bosses or clients. This may mean you could be asking someone who reports

to you to proof something as simple as a client email even if you have 25 years of experience in the industry. And they might even teach you something. Always be open to improvement.

2. **The first draft is never the final draft**

    It doesn't matter what level you are, deliverables will be refined by your own team and by clients and their stakeholders, and will evolve internally. Even if you think it's close to perfection the first time around, everyone wants to leave their mark. Remember, you are a consultant so inevitably there will be times when you're asked to make changes to deliverables you are passionately against. After providing your opinion and rationale a couple of times, your counsel may still be rejected and you will need to capitulate to senior members of the team or a client. Make sure to give in graciously, not begrudgingly, or you'll get a reputation that you're hard to work with.

3. **Assume what you write could go public**

    In this industry, we handle both confidential and sensitive information, often against the backdrop of political dynamics. Only write email, text, instant messenger, WhatsApp, Facebook messenger, WeChat, direct Tweet, and so on, content that you are happy to have forwarded to others or even published on the cover of *The Wall Street Journal*, *The Daily Mail*, or your favorite blog.

    To that end, be thoughtful, measured, objective, and accurate in all communication whether it's a pitch to a reporter, an email to a client, or an instant messenger chat with a colleague. You never know where or to whom your communication may be sent to or seen by.

    It's also critical to make sure documents containing sensitive information are clearly labeled "confidential," "draft," "for internal use only," and so forth, in the headers of your documents or emails in the unlikely event they are leaked. Your agency and/or client's general counsel can advise which language is best to use.

4. **Don't be seduced by spellcheck**

    Spellcheck is a great tool, but it doesn't pick up homonyms (words that sound the same but are spelled differently) or when you use the wrong word or tense altogether. (In one disastrous example, a book on PR had a few pages on "pubic relations." Yikes!) Use another person (preferably someone who has undergone proofing training or a professional sub-editor) to proof all client deliverables, including emails containing recommendations.

5. **Data check**

    Michael Bloomberg, former mayor of New York City once said "in God we trust, all others bring data." To that end, make sure all claims and content are referenced by primary sources (not Wikipedia!) and the citations are in the correct format for your sector (eg MLA (Modern

Language Association), APA (American Psychological Association), etc). Similar to proofing, have someone else check your work by matching up the claim and citation in the deliverable against the original reference to make sure all information is accurately represented and accounted for.

6. **Value quality control**

    Construct timelines so you always have time for deliverables to be reviewed, data checked, and proofed. If a client insists on a deadline that is too tight, it's critical to explain that the quality of the deliverable may be compromised if it can't undergo standard quality checks. It's never ideal to say "no" to a client, so ask them to reprioritize deliverable deadlines instead so you don't have to compromise the quality-control process.

7. **Finalize content first**

    Ask yourself, "What is the objective of this written material?" What you write should be serving that objective. It's likely that you are writing to either inform someone of something, such as a public disclosure, or persuade someone of something, such as a pitch to entice reporters to cover your client's story. In the event that what you intended to write will not help you achieve an objective, rethink whether it's even a necessary to draft. Content should always be serving an objective.

    When drafting content for email, we'll add that you should start your emails by writing and proofing all the content first, then add in the recipient's email address in the To, CC, or BCC lines. This may mean deleting email addresses while you are still working on your draft. Following this rule will prevent sending an email prematurely, which can help avoid embarrassing situations or even career devastating mistakes.

8. **Use an outbox delay**

    Ever rush to your sent file or outbox in a panic because you think you may have accidentally sent an email to the wrong person or just saw that your email crossed with one from your boss or client? Putting a few minutes' delay on outbound emails in your outbox can prevent anxiety by giving you a second chance to pull that email back.

9. **Feeling upset? Click "save" *not* "send"**

    A colleague sent you a passive aggressive text, a client sent you an angry email in caps, or you just got asked to fly halfway around the world in economy to work yet another weekend, and you have prepared a seething nasty-gram. Great, now hold all communication to avoid delivering the best retort you will ever regret. Revisit the potential communication when you've cooled off, and ask yourself what this communication is going to get you (other than a feeling of catharsis); is there something you can communicate that's more productive? Can you defuse the situation by picking up the phone or having an in-person chat instead? Do you need an outsider to step in to help defuse the situation? Or is it better not to respond at all? As we've already said, communication should be outcome focused.

10. **Be authentic**

    Remember that your online presence is often a substitute for "real life." If you would greet and leave a client in real life with a handshake, for example, make sure your email takes on that approach as well by using a salutation and farewell, such as "hello" and "best regards," respectively. That said, there's no need to be stiff and formal in professional correspondence as long as it's appropriate and not dotted with emoticons. People trust people, not robots, so be yourself.

References

Strunk, William, and E. B. White. *The Elements of Style.* Longman, 2000.

Zinsser, William. *On Writing Well: The Classic Guide to Writing Nonfiction.* HarperCollins, 2006.

Industry Insight

KRISTIN ENGDAHL ZIPAY

Vice president, Edelman
Washington, DC, USA

"All good writing is swimming underwater and holding your breath." The great F. Scott Fitzgerald had a point. No matter who you are, you'll need to work hard at writing. While most of us naturally began making the babbling sounds of speech in infancy, we need to be *taught* to write. It requires conscious effort and ongoing learning. In a busy agency environment, we tend to forget how much effort writing truly requires. I'm often asked to whip up an op-ed [article opposite the editorial page] at a moment's notice, or to incorporate a client's edits immediately, even if their feedback doesn't really make sense. Yet my days are filled with meetings, leaving little time for the quiet contemplation and time necessary for good writing. When clients are deadline-sensitive and colleagues are in a hurry too, it's tempting to overpromise, saying, "Sure, I'll draft that right away," even if you're not really sure how.

But being a good writer means standing up for what you need to do the job well. If I don't understand who I'm trying to reach with my writing or what I want them to think or do differently, I ask before diving in. Nothing is worse than making assumptions about such basic details, only to find out I wrote a perfect piece for an altogether irrelevant audience or purpose (it's happened).

I also set up my working environment to be most conducive to my creative muse and concentration. Even in an open-office layout, I find quiet space away from other distractions and put myself electronically on "do not disturb" mode. Ideally, if I can time it right or ask for a brief extension, I make use of the early morning hours when my brain is freshest – though my night owl colleagues prefer to work late into the evening after people leave the office. Whatever works!

Once I have a draft on paper, I rely on my colleagues to help me perfect it. Writing by committee can be a challenge, which is why, as the writer, I aim to maintain final editorial control when I can, rather than having someone yank the draft out of my hands, never to be seen again. But I fully admit I do need my colleagues' input and collaboration. We are all human; typos, grammatical mistakes, and convoluted sentence structures happen. No one is error-free; if you were, you'd be a robot, not a human. But that just means you're not on your own to figure out all the challenges of writing by yourself. You can learn a lot from a good editor if you're listening. The best editors don't only produce good writing – they produce good writers.

Throughout her 20-year career, Kristin has served as the go-to writer on her teams, crafting both long-form content such as speeches, and short-form material such as 150-word rapid-response letters to the editor. At Edelman, Kristin developed a "Common Sense Approach to Writing" curriculum to guide colleagues on how to effectively approach the writing process.

Part III

Forget Titles

Let's talk about what puts the "lead" in leadership. Did you know that to lead you don't need to be given a promotion or even permission? Recognize that everything you do is leading by example and you have the choice to hone how you use this power with every decision. Whether you're a student or a professional, this part will provide what you need to know to shift gears into a leadership mindset.

In this part, we will:

- dissect which behaviors make leaders successful;
- discuss why authenticity is critical to your career;
- provide tips to be diplomatic and persuasive;
- show you how to manage expectations effectively;
- explore why PR should stand for "personal relationships."

11 A Leader at Every Level

Leadership belongs to those who take it.

(Sheryl Sandberg)

Searching for "leadership books" on Amazon yields over 100,000 results – there's literally a book on every aspect of the topic from personal style to team motivation to business management and everything in between. This chapter is *not* going to attempt to summarize leadership because it's such a broad subject, means different things to different people, and almost everyone has an opinion.

However, there's one foundational principle that underlies most leadership teachings worth learning and that is to lead by example. When anyone says one thing and then does another, it erodes trust, and when people are distrustful, you never get the best out of them (Cardinal).

When should you start leading by example? This is the exciting part – you don't need to wait for anyone to grant you permission or give you a promotion (heck, you don't even need to have a public relations (PR) agency job yet!) to start leading by example right now in every facet of your life. The million-dollar question is – what example should you be setting?

According to *Harvard Business Review*'s (HBR) "CEO Genome Project" (Botelho et al), a 10-year study which analyzed leadership assessments of over 2,000 chief executive officers (CEOs), there are four behaviors that make leaders successful that you can practice right now, no matter what your level is or how many people you are leading (if any):

1. **Decide with speed and conviction**

    Perfectionism often holds us all back from making decisions every day, but if you want to be a successful leader, practice making decisions even if there's ambiguity, incomplete information, or you're in an unfamiliar domain. The trick is to balance the impact of getting a decision wrong versus the impact of not making a decision at all and causing a bottleneck. According to *HBR*, leaders who were described as "decisive" were 12 times more likely to be high performers even if some of their decisions were mistakes. And when you do make a mistake, be truthful about it and own it – that will help you earn respect at all levels from all levels.

2. **Engage for impact**

    Figure out what your stakeholders' priorities and motivations are and then influence them to move a goal forward. This could be applied to pretty much any interaction that requires persuasion and diplomacy (more on that in Chapter 13). Let's say your goal is to help make your team more effective by introducing a new editorial process. To do this, you're going to need to apply insights and communicate precisely with words and body language (60–90 percent of communication is non-verbal (Economy)) to instill confidence that this new process will be a success.

    The key to this practice is composure. Train yourself to stay cool under pressure by being completely mindful during these conversations and compartmentalizing any thoughts or feelings going on in the background. For example, let's say you just had a negative interaction with your boss and you're feeling irritated. If you act curt or defensive when your peers or direct reports raise objections to the new editorial process during the team meeting, it's going to be much harder to get them on board if they don't feel like their needs are viewed as valid or if they feel taken for granted.

3. **Adapt proactively**

    It's unlikely that you're ever going to face a situation directly out of a playbook, so it's essential to be able to think critically and laterally to mash up what you've learned and experienced to strategize, plan, problem solve, and execute. Instead of getting upset when a problem or challenge lands on your plate, be courageous and think of it as an opportunity to practice behaviors 1 and 2. Don't beat yourself up if you make mistakes along the way – CEOs who learned from their blunders had a 50 percent greater chance of thriving than those who considered setbacks failures.

4. **Deliver reliably**

    This is the most important behavior of all – following through on your commitments. The best way to be recognized as reliable is to manage the expectations of what you can deliver (see Chapter 14). There will inevitably be times when you will make a mistake and overcommit yourself, but it's better to do everything in your power to try to deliver anyway, especially if what you promised has high stakes. For example, it's much better to submit an important report to a client when you say you will even if that means pulling an all-nighter to get it done. CEOs who were assessed as reliable were twice as likely to land such a role in the first place and 15 times more likely to succeed in it.

Unfortunately, even if you deliver reliably 1,000 times in a row, the one time you don't, people will remember and it will affect your personal brand and reputation. With that said, even if that's how most people think – that's not how we recommend you should think. It's always better to give people the benefit of the doubt (Economy). Few people go into work with the intention to do a terrible job, let their teams down, and disappoint their clients.

As you can see from the HBR study, people are not born leaders, and the behaviors of the most successful leaders can be practiced now, regardless of age, role, title, specialty, or how many people work for you or with you. The more you behave like a leader, the more people will come to regard you as one.

References

Botelho, Elena Lytkina, Kim Rosenkoetter Powell, Stephen Kincaid, and Dina Wang. "What Sets Successful CEOs Apart." *Harvard Business Review*, May–June 2017, https://hbr.org/2017/05/what-sets-successful-ceos-apart.

Cardinal, Rosalind. "8 Top Ways to Lead by Example." *HuffPost*, 14 Mar. 2015, www.huffingtonpost.com/rosalind-cardinal/the-8-top-ways-to-lead-by_b_6446912.html.

Economy, Peter. "11 Remarkably Effective Ways to Lead by Example." *Inc.*, 9 July 2016, www.incarabia.com/lead/11-remarkably-effective-ways-to-lead-by-example/.

Industry Insight

CONROY BOXHILL

Managing director, Porter Novelli
Atlanta, Georgia, USA

PR agency life can be both exciting and challenging; it is certainly not for the faint of heart. And if you're a person of color, the struggle is real but you can do it. In the fast-paced, competitive agency environment, the most important thing you can do in your first six months is to pay attention to the rhythm of the organization. What behaviors do they value? What skills are valued or in demand? Do the people who are often celebrated share any characteristics or skills that are noticeable? The purpose of seeking these answers is to define for yourself the opportunities for growth in the organization and land mines that are important to avoid.

Looking back at the many ups and downs of my career, I would urge young professionals to spend time reading about leadership styles and perspectives. As elementary as it may sound, doing this consistently offers an invaluable way to develop and shape your analytical thinking and communications skills. While there's no substitute for experience, examples of leadership are published every single day. I learned this the hard way after being at my first agency job for three months. I was not a particularly good writer, at least for what was required of me to do my job effectively.

My manager at the time gave me some great advice. Since I couldn't afford to enlist in a writing class, he encouraged me to read articles from *The Wall Street Journal*, *New York Times*, and *Businessweek*, and select three each month that I would rewrite in my own words. It was life changing: my vocabulary expanded and I gained a much better understanding of what reporters were looking for. My advice to you is to use your consumption of media as a tool to build your core skills, your understanding of business and media, and how information is packaged and shared. You'll need this as you assume greater leadership roles.

Among the most important lessons I've learned in my career is that having a title does not equate to leadership. There are many opportunities to demonstrate leadership among your peer group, project team, and organization. The trick is to recognize those moments. Early in my agency career, my manager was taking me through my performance review; I was nervous but confident that I had worked hard and was deserving of a promotion. What I wasn't expecting is what he referenced as key proof points: he had observed me for months demonstrating the same level of respect for people at all levels of the organization – peers, juniors, and surprisingly the staff that cleaned the office at night. The lesson I learned was to recognize that people are always watching; offering respect and treating people with dignity is the single most important brick you can add to your career foundation. And before I forget, I got that promotion.

Conroy is a senior communications executive with diversified expertise across industries and disciplines. With more than 20 years of experience, his primary focus has been on helping brands build and protect their reputation.

12 Achieving Authenticity

> Be yourself; everyone else is already taken.
>
> (Oscar Wilde)

Who are you? What do you stand for? How do you want to be perceived? Yes, the soul-searching starts now. Whether it's your first day in public relations (PR) or your tenth year, you're going to end up in a position where a power dynamic with a client, colleague, or superior will make you feel that they have more authority or knowledge than you. Most people's automatic response is to stiffen up, be overly formal, polite, and agreeable, shamelessly suck up, and never ask questions.

We're going to let you in on a little secret: anyone with a shred of integrity is not going to trust, respect, or build rapport with a robot. This is why it's critical to your success to be authentic.

Take a minute and think about people who you respect and trust in your workplace, personal life, or even in the public sphere. What do they have in common? Probably that they are all comfortable in their own skin, emotionally intelligent, and live their values.

Get Comfortable in Your Own Skin

Whether you think you know yourself or you are still on the journey (I mean, aren't most of us?), it's important in PR (and in general) to be comfortable in your own skin so you speak and act genuinely. Whether you're currently a confident extrovert or an analytical introvert, own who you are. If you're comfortable in your own skin, you won't feel the need to change your demeanor to suit who you're engaging with. You'll always be evolving, but it's your core – the essence of your being – that you need to get comfortable with.

Easier said than done! This is going to sound rather "New Age," but the first step is to like yourself, even if it's just a little bit. If you're always beating yourself up for one thing or another, you're going to worry constantly, feel anxious, and then you're going to act mechanical in an attempt to not mess up an important interaction like a call with a client or a presentation to your agency's management. You need to embrace that you have qualities that are worthy of people's time.

"I'm not beating myself up," you might say. "I love myself and am awesome! I should have been promoted yesterday," you think. Okay – if you're that person, we're getting to you too, but you might love what we have to say next. The second step is to let go of the fear you won't admit you have. The fear that people won't like you or think you're good enough, smart enough, articulate enough, quick enough, and so on. There could very well be a basis for those fears, but we all have to work with what the universe doled out in parallel with any self-improvement efforts.

We're not saying you should be so self-congratulatory that you forget your team and tirelessly play devil's advocate. We are encouraging you to be at ease with yourself – both embracing your strengths and owning your growth areas – so other people can see the real you. And the secret that no one likes to talk about is that no one is perfect. So just be you.

The "real you" is where you'll have the greatest contribution, the greatest growth, and the greatest success. Even if it's not in the mold, what makes you different is what makes you special. While we haven't always been self-assured, we've developed confidence through experience – both the ups and the downs. Here are our top tips that we've shared with colleagues, and that we're now sharing with you.

- *Positive self-talk*

    Tell yourself you can and you will! If that's too cheesy for you or perhaps not concrete enough, make a list of your goals that you can hold in your hand; then create a strategy to achieve them. Whether you're stating goals for clients or for yourself, we strongly advise an accompanying strategy. Goals don't achieve themselves!

- *Don't believe your inner critic*

    Just because you have a negative thought, does that make it true? Question negativity that pops into your head and don't build on those thoughts – it gives them undeserved power.

- *Try meditating*

    A short meditation every day will help make you more aware of your thoughts and actions so you can cultivate positive thought patterns.

- *Get a mentor*

    Find someone inside or outside your agency (no one you work with directly) who will talk things out with you, hold you accountable to the changes you want to make, and give you a pep talk when you're sliding back into complacency. Kristin kept in touch with one of her first graduate school professors who guided her through many career decisions. Thirteen years later, this mentor is actually her current boss and has encouraged the writing of this book!

- *Prepare, prepare, prepare*

    If you're prepared for important interactions, odds are you're more likely to be yourself because you will replace nervousness or anxiety with confidence.

    Shalon has a tendency to speak quickly, so when she knows she has a major presentation (especially to people where English is not their first language), she'll record herself while she's practicing to make sure she delivers her ideas at a slower tempo.

- *Ask questions*

    If you don't know the jargon or don't understand an idea or concept being communicated, ask for clarification. This only works out if you prepare because if you ask questions you should already know the answer to, you may be written off as unhelpful and lose out on future opportunities.

- *Assert yourself, but don't dominate*

    Express your ideas and question ideas of others, but always engage in a productive dialogue. If you naturally dominate conversations, put down people's ideas, or interrupt others when they are speaking, knock it off. This helps no one, least of all you, who will be perceived as abrasive.

- *Show a genuine interest in others*

    Ask your colleagues and clients about their recent trips or kids or hobbies. This brings humanity into the workplace and will also help you see people and their varied expertise in new ways. Actively listen to the responses and find relevant ways to tie back into that.

- *Open up*

    People will trust you if they know more about you. Obviously, oversharing will have the opposite effect, but chatting briefly about the great hike you went on last weekend or providing recommendations to someone traveling somewhere you visited is a great way to establish rapport and show your interests. It may even lead to more opportunities for you. Kristin has always been passionate about public health – something she made no secret of – and it was precisely her openness about her passion that opened the door for her to be pursued for a plum agency role working on unbranded public health awareness campaigns.

Increase Your Emotional Intelligence

Emotional intelligence is that intangible quality that enables us to identify and manage our own emotions and the emotions of others (TalentSmart). It's difficult to know how much emotional intelligence you have and what to do if you find yourself in short supply. However, it's worth your time to try to figure it out. Decades of research have shown that 70 percent of the time, people with average IQs *and* high levels of emotional intelligence outperform people who only possess high IQs. In fact, 90 percent of top performers have high emotional intelligence (Bradbury; TalentSmart).

An analysis of results of over a million emotional intelligence tests administered by TalentSmart identified 11 indicators for lacking emotional intelligence (Bradbury):

- Not getting angry – masking emotions versus being genuine.
- Getting stressed easily.
- Difficulty asserting one's self.
- A limited emotional vocabulary.
- Making assumptions quickly and defending them.
- Holding grudges.
- Not letting go of mistakes.
- Feeling misunderstood.
- Not knowing one's triggers.
- Blaming other people for how one feels.
- Easily offended.

If you're identifying with any of the items on this list, then you may want to take an emotional intelligence test to pinpoint which aspect of emotional intelligence you probably need to work on – self-awareness, self-management, social awareness, or relationship management. A good starting point is the book *Emotional Intelligence 2.0* (Bradberry et al) that includes TalentSmart's scientifically validated emotional intelligence test (or you can take a free emotional intelligence test online for a sense check).

Toward the beginning of Shalon's career, she thought that building community inside an agency was a waste of time. She thought if she was her good-humored self, a direct communicator, acted with integrity, did amazing work, and her clients loved her, she would be on the fast track to senior management. *Wrong.* Taking the approach that "people politics" got in the way of performance – and overlooking team community-building – cost her a promotion and got her a free copy of *Emotional Intelligence 2.0* from her boss.

As a star performer, the situation felt incredibly infuriating and unfair. However, it was one of the greatest lessons Shalon learned professionally about raw authenticity, and she worked diligently to improve her emotional intelligence (after reading her free book), and both her career and personal relationships blossomed.

Don't wait for an emotional intelligence deficit to undermine your authenticity and career – put the denial aside and take action. Identify which areas of emotional intelligence you need to home in on, and then keep a journal of personal and professional interactions to help increase awareness of how you naturally respond, the reactions you receive, and the consequences of those interactions. By writing it down, you will be able to see as clear as day what you need to work on, and you can start to evolve your thoughts, perspectives, and ultimately your behavior to be more emotionally intelligent.

Live Your Values

In order to live by your values, you need to know what they are. Take a minute and write down five (or more) values that are important to you – what may help is thinking about how you would want friends, family, and colleagues to describe you in a eulogy. For example, we might want to be described as being authentic, knowledgeable, reliable, compassionate, loyal, and living with integrity and perseverance as our quirky selves. And, we'd want people to say we were fun to be around! (Who doesn't value fun?)

That was the easy part. Now you have to live by these values every minute of every day. Applying them when they're in your best interest is one thing, but aligning with your values when the going gets tough is what is going to earn you respect from yourself and those around you. Moreover, you will be challenged.

Kristin recalls far too many examples to mention when what she wanted to do and her values conflicted. An easy, yet unfortunate, example is the dreaded late-Friday request. These requests were extra special on holiday weekends, when after 4 pm the PR agency office is winding down and everyone is looking forward to three-day weekend luxuries such as travel, binge-TV-watching, or just family/friends time doing nothing. Right when the inbox is tidy and you think you're in the clear, you get a call or an email that your client needs you, but you desperately want to start your weekend . . .

Guess what? If your client needs you, that's a good thing. Though you might not want to do more work at 4 pm on a Friday, we'll reiterate: the client needs you. It means the client trusts you and relies on you. Further, if you're living by your values of being a reliable and trusted advisor, you will be there for your client. That's how it works. It may be the case that you spend simply 15 minutes on the phone to help the client assess the situation and find confidence that the request can wait, but it may also be the case that your client is in real crisis and managing the issue requires working over the long weekend.

Living your values will reinforce who you are and that will naturally cultivate authenticity. Doing great client work is not enough to succeed or become indispensable in a PR agency; authenticity is critical. However, authenticity must be cultivated and refined so you are comfortable in your skin, diplomatic, have mastery over your emotions, consideration for the emotions of others, and you walk your talk.

References

Bradberry, Travis. "11 Signs that You Lack Emotional Intelligence." *CNBC*, 28 Feb. 2018, www.cnbc.com/2018/02/28/11-signs-that-you-lack-emotional-intelligence.html.

Bradberry, Travis, Jean Greaves, and Patrick Lencioni. *Emotional Intelligence 2.0: The World's Most Popular Emotional Intelligence Test*. TalentSmart, 2009.

TalentSmart Inc. "About Emotional Intelligence." *TalentSmart*, 2018, www.talentsmart.com/about/emotional-intelligence.php. Accessed 22 May 2018.

Industry Insight

VERONICA MARSHALL

Creative instigator and purveyor of imagination
Washington, DC, USA

A senior leader I admire told me recently that I would have to choose between fitting in or alienating myself because people (okay, companies) don't want a trouble-maker. You see, I'm what they call a double outsider. I am black and a woman.

Early in my career, and even to this day, it was not uncommon to be the one and only person who looked like me or to walk into spaces that didn't reflect who I am. I have spent much of my career fighting to be seen, fighting to be heard, and fighting for opportunities for others. As a result, I was labeled difficult, angry, not a team player, and not a good "culture fit." I was excluded from opportunities that would have enabled me to advance more rapidly, or not considered for projects that would have enabled me to show people what I was truly made of.

At first, I hid my intelligence, ideas, personality – everything that made me authentic and real – because I didn't want to be labeled a trouble-maker. I worked diligently to fade into the background. But nothing about me can ever fade into the background. My laugh, big hair, expressive eyes, and animated stories make it impossible to do so.

While I may not know you individually, I am confident I know something about you personally. You are a disruptor, a fighter, an instigator, an original, and a change agent. No, I haven't read your LinkedIn profile, or perused your CV, or applauded your myriad accomplishments. I know this because you've picked up this book. In your own way, you are seeking new ways to stand out, and stand in your authenticity and power.

So, here's my advice. You belong there – that job, that meeting, that project. Never hide who you are or allow anyone to limit your beliefs and potential. Show up your full and complete self so you can knock down any barriers that will (oh, and they will) come your way. And don't be afraid to leap so you can achieve the things you've been told you can't. Leap in order to affirm who you are at the very core of your being. And leap so that you create spaces for others to walk into their authenticity and realness.

Creative instigator, original, and strategist connecting people with brands for the benefit of both, Veronica Marshall is no stranger to developing dynamic, integrated campaigns that solve human truths and tell compelling stories. She has worked on behalf of America's most recognized brands and celebrities, including: Wal-Mart Stores, Inc., M&M'S, Verizon, RITZ Crackers, DiGIORNO, Jay-Z, and Sean Combs.

13 Diplomacy and Persuasion

> Leadership is the art of getting someone else to do something you want done because he wants to do it.
>
> (Dwight D. Eisenhower)

Many of us grew up on the saying "honesty is the best policy"; and while that remains true, the way that "honest" remarks are communicated is often the difference between easily getting what you want and need out of a client or colleague or damaging your relationship. If you want to convince someone of something (persuasion), you're not going to get anywhere without mastering the art of being tactful and sensitive (diplomacy). This is important, because as an advisor you will need to understand the art of influence if you are: to convince clients that your idea will achieve their objective; to inspire your team to see the value of their contributions; or even to advocate for yourself as you grow your career.

Even if you pride yourself on being a direct communicator, you never have to say anything unkind to be honest or get what you want. In fact, the first thing you should ask yourself is whether what you want to communicate is even necessary and if it will get you closer to your objective. If the answer is "yes," then think about how you can communicate without evoking negative emotions in the other person. Whether we want to admit it or not, we all make decisions based on our emotions no matter how pragmatic and rational we think we may be.

There are countless books detailing techniques on diplomacy and persuasion if you're interested in the subject. However, here's five gems of advice that have served us well in the world of public relations (PR) agencies:

1. **Listen**

    You may not think you're making progress if you're not the one speaking, but that couldn't be more untrue. When people feel like they're being listened to (ie you're looking into their eyes), they're significantly more likely to trust you and be receptive to your ideas when it's your turn to speak.

Diplomacy and Persuasion 81

In addition to being a great tool to build rapport, listening is the best way to get what you want during a disagreement or negotiation. People are not comfortable with silence and will naturally fill the void. If you remain quiet, they will naturally elaborate (McCormack). The more someone talks, the more information and insight they are providing for you to use to your advantage later, and the less time they have to think about saying "no" to what you want, and plenty of time to talk themselves into unplanned concessions (McCormack).

However, if you skip this step and try to cut to the chase of what you want to talk about, it can come off as rude and uncaring even if it's because you only have five minutes left before your next meeting. It's always better to reschedule another time to connect and let the conversation drag on over a couple of calls or meetings than to rush the other person, get in a heated conversation, and escalate a simple dilemma into a full-blown issue or argument, which is not only personally unsavory, but can derail your client's project.

2. **Give consideration before disagreement**

    Most of the time we've made our mind up before the other person even utters their first word. Even if you follow the advice given in Gem 1 and listen until someone has finished speaking before voicing your disagreement, they will not think you actually *heard* them (Puhn). A calm discussion could escalate into a heated argument if you automatically disagree with an opinion.

    So, what's the best way to make someone feel heard and their contributions valued? Ask open-ended questions like, "What are your reasons for saying that?" – so you can weigh the pros and cons of their perspective (Puhn). You never know, this process may end up persuading you to see an issue differently!

3. **Use praise strategically**

    Every day there are dozens of opportunities to pay compliments to our bosses, colleagues, clients, friends, and family; yet most of the time we don't bother even though praise is free. Here's why you should start making the extra effort – when you sweeten your constructive criticism with praise, it primes the conversation and makes the other person more receptive to listening and acting on your critique (Puhn).

    However, if the only time you provide praise to someone is to punch them with a smile, give them a poo sandwich, or butter them up, it will be perceived as disingenuous and have the opposite effect. Compliments and praise must be truly sincere and deserved for this to work well, but the extra effort is worth it. It supports an environment where people feel safe to make mistakes and ask for feedback, which ultimately leads to fewer mistakes and more collaboration. Don't lose out on this powerful tool of persuasion by being stingy or lazy with compliments.

4. **Let them tell you "no"**

    We always thought that the more you get someone to say "yes" to you, the more they're going to say "yes," and then you get what you want. It was a complete revelation to learn that the more you let people say "no," the more comfortable they are with giving you what you want. Yes, you read that correctly!

    According to Chris Voss, an FBI hostage negotiator, trying to get people to tell you "yes" results in them feeling manipulated, eroding trust and rapport. "Yes" means commitment, which makes people twitchy, but saying "no" makes people feel like they've just protected themselves. When people feel protected, they relax and become more open and receptive (Barker).

    The key is to reword your questions to get a "no" instead of a "yes." For example, Shalon was in a situation where a creative partner was trying to pull out of a client commitment shortly before it was due. She called up her partner and the conversation went like this:

Partner: The scope of the project is more than I bargained for and I want to resign it.
Shalon: I understand you're frustrated with the situation, but do you want the client to think of your shop as unreliable?
Partner: No, of course not.
Shalon: Okay, so in your view, what's the most critical thing we need to do to salvage the project while taking the pressure off your shop?
Partner: We just need a shop or freelancer who can code within the client's budget.
Shalon: So, if we can find a developer who fits the bill this week, you won't need to resign the project?
Partner: That's right.

Voss claims that once the other party says the two magic words, "That's right," that's when you know they feel understood, they're no longer fighting you, and now you're collaborating. To get there, it's important to ask open-ended questions to uncover why the other person is resisting so you can start to problem solve (Barker).

5. **Earn your favors**

    As everyone's networks become larger and their lives busier, it becomes challenging to maintain consistent relationships even in your own workplace. However, this dynamic never makes it okay to ask for a favor before you've earned it – none of us likes to feel used.

    Imagine you've been working flat out on a client campaign for weeks – coming into the office early, staying late, maybe even coming in on the weekends. Your boss, who hasn't acknowledged any of this for ages and has missed your last three one-to-one weekly meetings because she's also swamped, stops by your desk and gives you a hurried compliment for keeping the client account afloat. Finally! Acknowledgment! In almost the same breath, she asks if you can fill in for her for an all-day meeting later in the week. How do you feel? Valued, or that she only pays attention to you when she needs something?

In a parallel universe, your boss stops by your desk every morning to ask how you're doing, apologizes for missing another meeting with you, and douses you in sincere praise for all your good work. Then, one afternoon, your boss presents you with a jar of your favorite chocolates – you know she must have thought about you on her last business trip because the chocolates are insanely expensive and only available to buy in person halfway around the world. Then she asks you the favor to stand in for her at an upcoming meeting. Are you more willing to help? Probably, because you feel cared about and empathize with the busy period you're both trying to get through.

People want to be treated like friends, not resources. They want to feel you care about their well-being, not just about what they can do for you. This applies to all of our relationships, including connections we make on LinkedIn. One of the best ways to earn favors is to keep in touch for sustained periods without asking for anything, and to be helpful if an opportunity presents itself.

While you could go through the motions of this advice to try to get ahead, practicing diplomacy with sincerity will naturally enable you to say the right thing at the right time to influence people and be persuasive. These tools will help you with the ultimate outcome of having stronger, more harmonious relationships with your clients and teams.

References

Barker, Eric. "7 Secrets for Being Super Persuasive, from an FBI Hostage Negotiator." *The Week*, 20 June 2016.

McCormack, Mark. *What They Don't Teach You at Harvard Business School*. Profile Books, 1984.

Puhn, Laurie. *Instant Persuasion: How to Change Your Words to Change Your Life*. Jeremy P. Tarcher/Penguin, 2006.

Industry Insight

JEFF MALDONADO

Managing director, KWT Global
New York, USA

One of the most fascinating and sometimes frustrating things about persuasion is that it's quite often also a *negotiation* – and this can be a tough pill to swallow for those new to the role of PR counselor. Over the course of my career, this has been one of the most important lessons that I've learned, and one that I've eagerly tried to impress upon my teams. While there'll be moments where you'll have to counsel firmly to avoid reputational missteps (or worse), more often than not you'll be presented with moments where persuasion via negotiation done right will help build your credibility and make your communication programs stronger and more sustainable – while also ensuring the other party feels like they have skin in the game.

In these moments, practitioners must embrace the long game of persuasion, and in some of my most successful client negotiations it starts with *empathy* – understanding not only what your client wants but the underlying currents that brought them to that very point. For example, are there personal or political (internal) implications or other underlying emotions that may be coloring their request? We see this regularly with clients – believe it or not, they're human, too! It's here that a practitioner must be comfortable digging deeper to fully understand the depth of counsel required, as well as the give and take needed to navigate the negotiation to persuade effectively.

At my firm, we borrow quite a bit from the practice of "design thinking," and have always been fascinated by this quote from legendary industrial designer Dieter Rams: "Indifference towards people and the reality in which they live is actually the one and only cardinal sin of design." An argument can be made that this, too, is the one and only sin of good communication and, as such, effective persuasion.

Beyond client counsel, however, mastering the art of the negotiation is arguably most critical to intra-agency dynamics. Like most progressive agencies today, we have three *very* distinct generations represented, each with their own unique worldview and approach. While I'd love to say we get along all the time and that our commonalities outweigh our differences, again – we're human! Being empathetic to one another serves as a bridge that can smooth out misunderstandings before they arise and allows us to collaborate effectively. I've witnessed that putting this into practice internally is particularly important to teams that must weather client crises together (which is almost always), especially when following specific directions and navigating heightened emotions are critical to success both short and long term.

For more than 14 years, Jeff has lent his hybrid marketing and communication expertise to clients across a range of industries, with specialties in corporate/business-to-business (B2B), enterprise technology, innovation, and telecommunications. With deep expertise in both analog and digital PR, and a progressive approach to business leadership, Jeff and his teams help build truly integrated, insights-driven programs for clients.

14 Managing Expectations

> The single biggest problem in communication is the illusion that it has taken place.
>
> (George Bernard Shaw)

If you follow the five rules of managing expectations, you will avoid the dreaded "D" word, *disappointment*. Wait a second, a little disappointment never really hurt anyone, right? You may think it's just an emotion that will pass, but it can wreak havoc on your professional and personal relationships.

Imagine for a minute that you just went through three rounds of grueling interviews and landed your public relations (PR) dream job. Better yet, they offered the exact salary you wanted – you didn't even have to negotiate! You couldn't be happier. Fast forward three months – you're working hard, getting on brilliantly with your boss and all of your colleagues. Then, you find out that someone with the same qualifications, years of experience, age, and gender as you is making $10,000 more a year for the same role. How do you feel about your job now?

Your gut reaction is probably that the situation is unfair. But why? Didn't you get exactly what you wanted? The difference between life before you realized your peer was making $10K more than you and life after is expectations. Once your expectation was reset, the happiness and contentment you felt went up in smoke. As you can see with this example, there's no coming back from disappointment, which is why it needs to be avoided like the plague.

What we accept in business and in life isn't necessarily good or bad – we accept what aligns with the expectation established. You could deliver the best work product in the world; however, if it's not what the client wanted, they're still going to be disappointed. The work is important, but managing expectations is paramount. It builds trust and your reputation. Trust is simply the outcome of promises – or expectations – fulfilled. Don't ever let a gap form between what stakeholders think they're going to get and what you're actually able or willing to deliver.

The Five Rules of Expectation Management

1. **Delete the phrase "under-promise and over-deliver" from your mind and vernacular**

    If you consistently under-promise and then over-deliver, you form the expectation that you will *always* pull a rabbit out of your hat no matter what.

    We urge you to be realistic and honest when negotiating project metrics, deadlines, budget, and so forth, so you remain in control of your stakeholders' expectations. They need to take what you say at face value, otherwise they will develop their own set of expectations (probably false ones) based on your past behavior.

2. **Only say "yes" if you mean it**

    If your boss asks you to leave your vacation early to fly to a meeting halfway around the world, do not agree unless you are genuinely happy to do it or can negotiate some type of concession to make it worthwhile (such as a few days of vacation in that destination, for example). If a client begs you to turn something around in 24 hours, but you know that unless there is a divine miracle, it isn't possible, do not agree to it.

    Once you agree to something, you set an expectation that you will deliver. If you try to get out of it:

    a. you will beat yourself up for agreeing because you already know the reality is that you don't want to or can't do it;
    b. your thoughts will be dominated by trying to weave some elaborate tale;
    c. it's likely the tale you weave is a bold-faced lie or pathetic excuse and it's in direct opposition with the values you're striving to live by;
    d. it's likely that this will lead to the other party being disappointed, losing trust in you, and potentially losing respect for you (depending on what the ask was and how you tried to get out of it).

    You can easily avoid this downward spiral by not agreeing to anything on the spot if you have even a shred of hesitancy. Tell the other party you need to think about it and/or check with a relevant person to see if it is possible – buy yourself time so you can think clearly without the pressure of someone standing over you.

3. **Never say the word "no"**

    In the era of "Me Too," we have to acknowledge that "never say 'no'" can pull anyone to attention. We are speaking about this only in the spirit of expectation management for non-threatening business requests, of course. And to the degree you're asked to do something that isn't within your capacity or timeline, then we urge you not to say "yes" . . . but don't say "no" either. Let us explain.

    It doesn't matter what words you say around the word "no" to justify or soften it, your boss will still perceive you as not being a team player or, worse, as "difficult"; your clients will think you don't want to help them and don't care about their accounts, and your colleagues will think you don't have their backs.

"But wait," you're thinking. "Didn't you just tell me not to say "yes" unless I mean it? What if I actually don't want to do something or know I can't do something?" We hear you. Let's go back to the examples from Rule 2 for a minute: your boss asks you to leave your vacation early to go to a meeting. Go back to your values to negotiate your way out of the situation or into a better one. No one with integrity is going to ask you to break your values. So, in this circumstance, you may say something to the effect that you already made a commitment to your spouse/kids/friends that you would be there and it's important to you to honor all of your commitments inside and outside of work. Further, that you know integrity and dependability are some of your boss's core values too (or even core values of the agency).

Now for the client example – your client wants a new infographic turned around in 24 hours so she can capitalize on a trend on social media. You know the art director is out sick and the graphics team is slammed with other work, some of which is for that client. What not to do? Don't tell the client that you or creative have deadlines for other clients. It's critical to the success of your relationship that they always feel like they're the only client even though they know they're not.

Therefore, what should you do? Explain that while you can accomplish everything, it can't all be done at the same time. Ask the client to prioritize which deliverable is most important for this week – if you squeeze in the infographic, X, Y, and Z will need to be delayed until next week, is that okay? Almost every time, the client will say, yes. Or, if the client says no, then explain that you will deliver, but the quality may suffer because the team will have to rush, or it won't be designed properly, or it won't be proofed or data checked, and so on. Show the client you're willing to help, but that a sudden urgent request will have an impact on the work if he or she won't reprioritize the workflow.

If clients beg you to do something that you cannot reasonably do, and you give in, and you do magically manage to pull everything off and to a high standard, then we're back to Rule 1 – they will always think you can pull a rabbit out of the hat. They will not, however, understand or appreciate how many favors you had to call or how much stress you had to endure to make it happen. It will simply be the new expectation.

The trick is to master the art of saying "no" without ever actually uttering the word. By not saying the word, "no," you're communicating that you want to help (even if you are unable to) and that will make all the difference to how you are perceived. How you are perceived will affect your ability to set realistic expectations while preserving your relationships.

4. **Build consensus**

    Have you ever left a group call or meeting and everyone has a different idea of what's supposed to happen next or what the key takeaway was? Most interactions have plenty of room for misunderstandings. It is critical that you clearly gain consensus and specificity of deliverables, deadlines, metrics, or results to make sure that everyone is moving in the same direction and there will not be mismatched expectations later.

    For example, the client may say they want "good" media coverage for an upcoming announcement and you agree that's achievable because it's a great story. While the trade publications didn't end up being particularly interested, you secured a cover story in *The New York Times*. Amazing, right? You excitedly call up your client team to deliver the news and then you hear it in their voice – disappointment. They were expecting a high volume of trade features. You hang up bewildered – doesn't everyone value top-tier coverage above all else? Not necessarily . . . and that gap between what the client wanted and what you delivered led to disappointment even though you technically did a great job.

    To establish consensus on a call or in a meeting, ask people individually if they're on board with "X," or recap that what you think you heard is that we're all going to do "Y," and ask anyone to chime in if they disagree. If you're only speaking to one person, tell them you're going to recap the ask to make sure you understand.

5. **Put it in writing**

    The quickest way to diffuse a disagreement or nip disappointment in the bud over unmet expectations is to bring proof of the original expectation. We are all drowning in information daily, so it would not be far-fetched for an expectation to evolve over time based on what we thought we heard or remembered, even if there seemed to be consensus at the time. This is why you need to put everything in writing as soon as it's been agreed upon and, if a lot of time passes, to remind the other party (gently!) of the agreed upon expectation. This doesn't have to be a formal document or contract, it can be as simple as meeting minutes or an informal recap email to remind everyone of what was agreed at the onset.

Since instant communication often exacerbates poor decision-making, make your first priority to learn how to create space so you can critically think how you're going to respond. Once you have the time to think requests through, the rules will become second nature – if you can think clearly, you can act clearly.

Industry Insight

ALI GEE

Senior partner and deputy chief executive officer (CEO), FleishmanHillard Fishburn
Member of the Chartered Institute of Public Relations (CIPR)
London, United Kingdom

Managing expectations should be a part of every agency consultant's day, however senior they are. At the junior level, it's simply about ensuring that your client knows what to expect and, by taking control of this, making sure you match it or, if possible, exceed it.

Clients have a canny habit of increasing the scope of a campaign or project as it goes along. By continually referring back to the agreed scope and deliverables, agency teams can avoid this becoming a source of contention in the future. So, it's about being clear about what they're paying for and reducing the chances of conflict occurring in the agency-client relationship.

But it's not just about clients. Your team mates, your bosses, and your partners all need to be clear about what you're going to deliver. Agency-side, this is often about meeting deadlines. Your life will be one huge juggling act of client and colleague demands. Be reasonable about what you can achieve in the time you have to do the job. Say "yes," put your hand up to "take it on," but make sure you're not committing to more than you can realistically pull off.

Finally, start out as you mean to go on. These conversations work best at the beginning of a relationship. In my past, in an effort to delight newly won clients or even prospects who haven't yet signed on the dotted line, I've found myself giving the impression that there's an endless commitment to "always on" service and support. I've learned that this rarely ends well. Either the client ends up feeling like what was promised at pitch didn't materialize, or the agency massively overservices a piece of work in order to live up to the promise.

The lesson is this: be realistic and truthful about what your clients and colleagues can expect. It's the basis on which long-term relationships thrive.

Ali's PR career spans 25 years, almost all of which has been spent agency-side. She has worked at the world's largest and smallest agencies in the UK and USA. Prior to joining FleishmanHillard Fishburn, Ali was CEO at Omnicom agency Fishburn and before that, EVP at Edelman. Her specialism is planning and strategy.

15 PR: Personal Relationships

> I speak to everyone in the same way, whether he is the garbage man or the president of the university.
>
> (Albert Einstein)

Let's clear the air: PR does not mean "press release." While anyone reading this book knows that already, it's less certain that people outside of our industry realize that public relations (PR) is more than media relations, more than events, and much more. Although we're all in agreement that PR is more, it's trickier to find agreement among those practicing public relations on what PR precisely is, since it encompasses so much.

We're going to define PR from two perspectives: 1) what it means for the industry; and 2) what it means for you, as a PR consultant.

Defining PR: In Industry

The Public Relations Society of America (PRSA), the largest professional communication organization in the USA, defines public relations as: "a strategic communication process that builds mutually beneficial relationships between organizations and their publics." The key word in this definition is "relationships."

To understand the role of relationships in our industry, we have to take a peek back in time when the profession of PR was first developed. Edward L. Bernays is most credited with conceiving "public relations" as a professional discipline. In fact, he's often referred to as "The Father of Public Relations." Bernays, the nephew of the famous psychologist Sigmund Freud, saw opportunity in understanding how people think and influencing that thinking to shape what people do (Brinson). He authored and published a seminal book on this topic in 1923 called, *Crystallizing Public Opinion*.

As a PR advisor to many corporations and heads of state, Bernays developed what today is a multi-billion-dollar industry simply by understanding how people think and by shaping behavior. He called it the "engineering of consent" (Bernays). Psychology and strategy play principle roles in this – but what is essential to the success of PR are the personal relationships that inspire change in public opinion.

One shining example of this is Bernays' "Torches of Freedom" campaign (Brinson). In 1928, Bernays was approached by the president of the American Tobacco Company to open a new market: women. At the time, it was only acceptable for men to smoke cigarettes, which meant tobacco companies were missing out on a big percentage of the market. While there was a small and growing population of women who smoked cigarettes, most women wouldn't dare smoke in public. There was significant stigma around smoking – for social reasons, rather than the health reasons we know today, which were still unknown at the time. Any woman who lit up in public was labeled undignified, sexually suggestive, and worse. (Keep in mind the Nineteenth Amendment, giving women the right to vote, had only passed in 1920 so there was a lot of work to be done on the gender equality front.) Bernays saw, however, the mutually beneficial opportunity this presented: tobacco wanted female consumers, and women wanted more freedoms and equality. Reveal: Torches of Freedom.

In an impressively orchestrated PR campaign, Bernays alerted media to a "scandal" that would take place at the height of the well-attended, respectable, Easter Day Parade along Fifth Avenue in New York City. And he delivered: a lovely young woman by the name of Bertha Hunt, who also happened to be Bernays' secretary, unapologetically lit up her Lucky Strike cigarette. In a dramatic fashion, Bernays had arranged for additional women to follow Hunt with their cigarettes, creating a public defiance to the patriarchy and elevating the cigarette to a symbol of women's liberty. The media pounced and the rest is PR history.

This case study is more than just a stunt. It highlights how understanding a stakeholder's psychology and the complex relationships at play can influence behavior. In this case, relationships among women – and their relationship with the cigarette first as a stigma and then as a symbol of power – contributed to an entire social movement. According to PRSA, "public relations is about influencing, engaging and building a relationship with key stakeholders across a myriad of platforms in order to shape and frame the public perception of an organization." Fundamentally, public relations is about personal relationships.

Defining PR: In Your Career

We've established that effective PR is fundamentally the successful management of relationships for clients. But what about you? Who is doing your PR? Yes – you have relationships to manage as well, and it will benefit you greatly to take the same skills you exercise for your clients and bring them into your own career management. Help inspire others to see you as you would like to be seen so that you can get the opportunities you'd like to get.

Here's a brutal truth: people get jobs because, somewhere along the way, someone with influence liked them. However small, there was a relationship at play. The technical skills, the experience, and the credentials are supremely important, but guess what? There are 10 people in line with the equivalent skills, experience, and credentials. The way you will stand out – and ultimately advance – is with your ability to build relationships.

Building relationships takes work, but there are three ways to be better at this in your career.

1. **Care**

    The simplest "how to" can be summed up in one four-letter word: care. "Care" is almost impossible to teach – but if you have it within you to seek the value in what you're doing and why you're doing it, then a real connection with your work might just reveal itself. You don't have to be living your life's passion, but find a reason to appreciate whatever it is that you're doing, as well as the work of others. We know from psychology that people are drawn to others who care.

    At one agency, Kristin recalls that a colleague worked on a constipation relief account. Yep – all day, a team got to work with their pharma client on a drug to help people poo. Many people would think that account stinks (pun intended!), but Kristin's colleague loved working on that account. Though there weren't any sexy celebrity campaigns or glossy events in the mix, there was purpose. Kristin's colleague explained that many people living with chronic disease, such as late-stage cancer patients, often take opioid drugs to manage severe and debilitating pain. One of the unfortunate side effects of this, however, is painful and dangerous constipation. Though we're in PR, not medicine, the woman working with this constipation relief account saw her role in promoting the drug as helping to ease suffering. She cared. She was a better client advisor because of it, she managed a stronger and more unified team because of it, and people were drawn to her because, well, she was exceptional and she cared.

2. **Contribute**

    There are many ways to contribute, and if you've taken the time to care, they'll be apparent to you. It may mean that you spend an hour mentoring someone with less experience, or staying an hour late to learn from someone who's done it all before. It might mean making the first outreach for that lunch date that never happens, versus waiting for the other person to reach out to you. It might mean pitching a new idea, setting aside extra time, or putting in the extra polish. It might even mean spending months of your life writing a book in the hopes that you can make someone's life easier than yours was (oh wait, are we projecting!?). What it always means is extra work. However, if you care, you will be inspired to contribute anyway. On the plus side, contributing ultimately means extra rewards, both intrinsic and tangible.

The tricky thing about doing your own PR for personal relationships is that the reward is not always apparent. It may be that relationships don't do anything to support you in the short term. But the industry is small. Down the line, when reputation and trust are your currency, good relationships are like money in the bank because the reputation and the trust are already established. One very important note on this: relationships aren't transactional. The relationship is the goal – not what the relationship can do for you. You shouldn't do things for others simply because you want something in return. The "return" is the likely and natural consequence of your contributions but should not be confused as the motivation.

3. **Be consistent**

Building trust and relationships through consistent performance is an easy formula: say you'll do something + do it = consistency.

Consistency isn't only about delivering mega client results and it doesn't have to be about big projects either. In fact, the little things you do for your agency team on a regular basis can have a big impact.

For example, many PR professionals starting out in their career will be asked to monitor for news or social media coverage and to create reports. Referred to as "media monitoring," this is a tedious task that can take hours of someone's day, and these reports are routinely requested. Go to any agency and mention "media monitoring" to a junior account professional and you'll hear an audible, "ugh!" It's typically at the bottom of everyone's list of favorite projects. (It doesn't even make the list, if we're being honest.)

Yet what the task lacks in glamour and excitement it makes up for in value and substance. Clients rely on these reports to understand the impact PR is having on their business and often leverage the reports to market the importance of their function and secure funding for additional projects they want to give to your agency. Media monitoring reports are incredibly important to clients and, therefore, the person entrusted with this seemingly menial task is playing a vital role on the account team. This person has to be sure to capture all coverage, format it correctly into a report, analyze it, and get it to a reviewer by a deadline. Every day. This takes time management, insight, and precision. Doing this well every single day builds your reputation – many people rely on you. Doing this well means you're making your reviewer's job easier by meeting the deadline and having a (near) perfect draft, and you're making your agency look good by creating a product that the client values. We know you didn't go to college to copy and paste news articles – but it's the perfect example of how performing consistently will make you stand out.

In summary, PR has many definitions but, at the core of it all, it's about personal relationships. This is as true for the client's work with stakeholders as it is for you with your "stakeholders," whether they are bosses, co-workers, clients, prospective employers, industry peers, or others.

References

Bernays, Edward L., and Howard Walden Cutler. *The Engineering of Consent. Howard Walden Cutler and Others*. University of Oklahoma Press, 1955.

Brinson, Carroll. "Edward L. Bernays: Founder of Professional Public Relations." *The Mississippi Business Journal (Pre-Aug 20, 2012)*, vol. 8, no. 4, 1986, p. 7.

Public Relations Society of America, Inc. (PRSA). "All About PR." *Public Relations Society of America*, 2018, www.prsa.org/all-about-pr/.

Industry Insight

BRIAN N. LEE, APR

President, Revelation PR, Advertising & Social Media
Madison, Wisconsin, USA

If you've ever been to a networking event, conference, or social mixer, then you may be familiar with the following situation. You meet someone, and within 10 seconds you realize that they'll never do business with you. In other words, that person is not your prospect. However, I'm hesitant to abandon the conversation because I'm in the mindset of building relationships. When someone deems you as trustworthy, competent and, frankly, a decent person, then they'll provide you with other things you covet – insights, leads, and/or referrals.

One of my first clients came this way. I had gotten to know a lawyer whose firm wasn't looking to outsource its PR or marketing. However, he happens to also own several buildings, and one of his restaurant tenants was not doing well. He introduced me to the owner, who ended up hiring me to rebrand the restaurant. Many well-connected people in the city knew of the turnaround, and that led to additional referrals. The lawyer and I stay in touch, and as a result, he has provided subsequent opportunities for me.

You never know who's in any person's particular network, and you never will know unless you nurture relationships. The keys are building your reputation in a non-egotistical way, providing value to others whenever possible, and not selling.

Brian is the president of Revelation PR, Advertising & Social Media and a part-time lecturer on social media at Madison Area Technical College. A graduate of the University of Wisconsin, Brian has also served on the national board of directors for PRSA and Ad 2, and is the author of Using Social Media for Business.

Part IV

Lead the Way

If you think you stop "doing" when you become a middle manager (managers to senior vice presidents) or even a director, you are mistaken – your role just becomes complex. You're expected to manage, lead, and do. When you're in middle management, it's an ongoing challenge to dedicate enough headspace to leading unless you've built a fantastic team to support you. Whether you've recently been promoted to account management or have been in middle management for a while, this part will provide practical advice to bring out the best in your management and leadership style against the backdrop of a demanding workload.

In this part, we will:

- explore building a solid team;
- discuss developing and maintaining your personal brand;
- explain managing your career trajectory;
- unpack how to be an impactful mentor;
- get into the nuts and bolts of managing client relationships.

16 Building a Team

> In most cases being a good boss means hiring talented people and then getting out of their way.
>
> (Tina Fey)

How to Build a Team

Building a solid team is like a chemical reaction: if you get all the elements right, you end up with a useful solution; if you get the proportions wrong, you end up with a mess. So how do you know who to pick to get it right? In this chapter, we're going to dive into all the considerations of what success looks like.

First, we need to pinpoint the goal. The most important question you need to ask yourself is – what does this team need to achieve? For example, if the client's goal is to raise awareness of a specific disease area, and they're going to use media hits and social media engagement as a proxy to measure a perceptual shift, this tells you a lot about the skillsets needed in order for the team to succeed.

When you think about building a team, your mind may immediately jump to people who you perceive to be "good" or people with capacity who are available to do the work. While it may seem counterintuitive, you're not going to build a solid team if you start with specific people. Instead, start with a list of the must-have skillsets to deliver the scope and achieve the client's goals.

To continue with our example of disease awareness, here's a list of potential skillsets that would be needed.

- Subject-matter expertise – knowledge/experience of the specific disease area
- Research/insights
- Strategy
- Graphic design
- Copywriting
- Paid social

- Organic social/community management
- Media relations
- Advocacy
- Measurement
- Project management

Once you know what you need, you can start thinking about the specific individuals who have each of these core competencies (Table 16.1).

Now, it's time to think about the added value each person brings to the table as well their limitations (Table 16.2). Is someone amazing at their job, but a procrastinator who will stress out the rest of the team? It's important to think about how each person will operate with the rest of the team. You could select individuals who are fantastic at their respective area of expertise, but if there's political dynamics or a clash in values, it could easily prevent the team from working well as a whole.

In this case, most of the best performers have an issue with time management; however, since David is an assertive and skilled project manager, he should be able to balance out many of the team's limitations by orchestrating the timelines. Overall, no one has a major personality conflict, although Diana and Mike may perceive David's attempts to hold them accountable as a personal critique. Even an ideal team isn't going to get along with each other 100 percent of the time, but the more harmonious the relationships are, the more work the team will be able to accomplish because they won't be distracted by interpersonal issues.

Next, we need to figure out if we can actually afford our ideal team based on how much of their time is needed, their hourly rates, and the client's budget of $175,000 (Table 16.3).

Table 16.1 Team Member Skillsets

Team Member	Primary Skills	Secondary Skills
Sam	Communications strategy	Subject-matter expertise
Diana	Creative strategy	Video production
Harry	Graphic design	Animation
Amanda	Copywriting	Organic social/community management
Tom	Research/insights	Measurement
David	Advocacy	Project management
Sally	Paid social	Organic social/community management
Mike	Media relations	Blogger relations

Table 16.2 Team Member Added Value versus Limitations

Team Member	Added Value	Limitations
Sam	Team cheerleader Great presenter	Often harried because he's working with several clients
Diana	Funny Bolsters team morale	Difficulty accepting feedback to evolve ideas
Harry	Works efficiently	Requires specific brief – won't take an idea and run with it
Amanda	Proof-reading/sub-editing skills	Always spends more time than she estimates
Tom	Logical Detail-oriented	Known for missing internal deadlines
David	Proactive Direct communicator Organized	Strong-headed
Sally	Reliable and excellent performer under pressure	Overly laid-back attitude Procrastinator
Mike	Kind Jovial	Sensitive – takes feedback personally

Table 16.3 Ideal Team Billing Cost

Team Member	Hours Needed	Hourly Rate	Cost
Sam	70	$250	$17,500
Diana	70	$185	$12,950
Harry	200	$120	$24,000
Amanda	200	$100	$20,000
Tom	150	$75	$11,250
David	300	$140	$42,000
Sally	250	$100	$25,000
Mike	250	$120	$30,000
Total			$182,700

Our current team is $7,700 over budget. There are a couple of things we could do. For starters, we could figure out if someone we know to be extremely efficient, like Harry, can perform the scope in fewer hours. Another approach would be to think about other colleagues with lower billing rates who may be able to do some of the work. For example, if we cut Mike's hours by half – from 250 to 125 hours – and provided him with a rising star in media relations who bills at $75 to help with media sell-ins and coordinating interviews, we would be able to reduce the cost of the team by $5,625. This revised team mix will be close enough to the client's budget to make it work.

Where building a team can get tricky is before the team is officially allocated – a team member who was available yesterday may suddenly be pulled on to an urgent project or traded during a capacity planning meeting, which completely changes that person's workload and availability.

For illustrative purposes, let's say that David was pulled into a new business pitch and won't be able to give as much of his time as we originally planned for. Yikes! He's the glue keeping the team together! What do we do? Well, part of his role is advocacy, so let's try to find someone else with a similar billing rate who can take on that role so David can focus what time he does have on project management. Oh no, you just found out that David won't work on the account unless he gets to own the advocacy piece. What do you do now?

At this point, you can either persuade David to take the role on anyway because that's what's best for the agency (although it may not be what's best for his own career trajectory), or you can look for another person to fulfill the project management role who has the same added value as David. Since David is the glue holding this particular team together and is in a position to say "yes" or "no" to his role on a team, if an assertive and skilled project manager cannot be found, the rest of the team may need to be re-evaluated (ie replace the people who struggle with time management even if you prefer their other skills or style). Keeping to timeline and budget is critical to a project being perceived as a success. Furthermore, it will be very difficult to convince a client to believe that the team will achieve the goals if they can't submit day-to-day deliverables on time or budget.

Although this process may be the best practice for building a team, you may often find yourself managing or leading a team where you didn't get to pick the people. It's still worthwhile to go through the process of thinking about each person's core competencies, added value, and limitations. It's critical to identify as early as possible if you have the mix of skillsets to succeed. If you find your team coming up short, flag this to your boss as soon as possible. In most cases, if you make a pragmatic argument about your team mix, the powers that be will help you get the resources you need to be successful whether that's trading staff with another team, borrowing a resource from a sister agency, or even hiring someone new.

Hiring

From our agency experience, hiring can sometimes be a chaotic and unstandardized process. Once financial sign-off for a new hire is secured, the process often devolves to the hiring practices that you would expect at a start-up. Human resources (HR) or a recruiter digs up candidates to be interviewed, the job descriptions are often templates, candidates interview with whoever is available, questions are asked at random, and offers are made quickly to people who are liked.

During one of Shalon's agency experiences, the managing director (MD) was resistant to hiring the seasoned talent needed to build a functional team because it would lower the profit margins of the account. The MD's solution was to hire half a dozen new university graduates. Since Shalon disagreed with the approach, the MD would surprise her with batches of these new hires whenever Shalon returned from a business trip. The resulting staff mix precipitated a very stressful dynamic for Shalon and her team because there weren't enough experienced hands to do the client work and teach the newbies – not a fair or good experience for anyone.

Needless to say, we prefer a much more thoughtful approach to hiring. Once you've thought through the staff mix and identified the skillset gaps and the budget available to fill those gaps, you have a clear idea of what level professional you need to hire and the cross-section of experience and traits you need them to have for the team to function effectively to achieve the client's goal.

Our advice is to work with HR and your boss to draft a specific job description and to put together a list of interview questions and a rubric that will help you: 1) to identify whether the candidate has the right skills and experience to fulfill your need; and 2) to compare candidates in a more standardized way so you're not making hiring decisions based on your gut feeling that he or she will be a rock star (although that does come into it).

Let's say HR has lined up five interview candidates to fill the role you had originally planned for David. So, you're looking for a candidate at the account director level with 6–8 years of disease awareness and advocacy experience (preferably in the disease area they will be working on), project management experience, and excellent communication and organizational skills. Simply asking a candidate to walk you through their résumé is not going to reveal to you everything you need to know.

Below are the questions we would ask in this scenario (many of which can be refined and applied to interview candidates of other specialties and levels). It's a good rule of thumb to kick off the interview with a few pleasantries to make the candidate comfortable before starting your questions. While you will be asking a list of questions, make sure you ask follow-up questions to get more details and to make the interview more like a conversation – this is how you'll obtain good quality information. Also, use the power of silence – let them keep talking and talking to fill the awkward void so they reveal themselves to you. This is where you will get most of the critical information that will inform your decision.

- What made you interested in this particular account director position?
- Why did you leave your last position?
- Tell me about your experience in X disease area. What type of work did you do and what were you responsible for?
- Which disease awareness campaign on your résumé are you most proud of and why?
- What was the goal of the campaign and what were the results?

- If I called your client after this interview, what do you think they would tell me about the campaign?
- Which advocacy relationships were critical to the success of the campaign and how did you get them on board? (And follow-up: what were the challenges you faced?)
- Can you tell me about an experience during this campaign where something was not going to plan and what you did to resolve the situation?
- Walk me through your project management process for this campaign. How did you keep the team organized?
- What's your approach to managing client expectations?
- How do you ensure campaigns are delivered on time and on budget?
- Tell me about a time when it looked like a deliverable wasn't going to be submitted on time to a client – what did you end up doing?
- What would you do if a team member missed a deadline?
- How do you deliver constructive feedback?
- Tell me about a time when a project went off-budget – how did you handle it with your boss, team, and client?
- What would you do if someone on the team diverged from your project management processes or had ideas to improve the process?
- Tell me about a time when you had a difference of opinion with a client – how did the situation conclude?
- Tell me about a time when you had a conflict with someone with a higher title or more years of experience than you.
- Tell me about a time when you had a conflict with someone who reports to you and how you handled it.
- What are your three greatest strengths and three greatest weaknesses?
- If I called your boss after this interview, what would they tell me?
- If I called the most junior member of your last team, what do you think they would say about you?
- Everyone gets along with some types of people more than others; what are the characteristics you get along with best?
- What do you want to get out of your career in the next year and in the next three years?
- What are the top three things you're looking for in your next employer?

Interviews are as much about you selling the position and your agency to the candidate as they are about the candidate selling themselves to you. Make sure you give a compelling but honest description of what the job will be like day to day, opportunities for growth, client relationship, and agency culture.

To conclude the interview, ask "Do you have any questions for me?" If the candidate doesn't have any questions, that means they lack intellectual curiosity, will be a yes-person, and/or didn't prepare properly for the interview. If the candidate only asks questions about salary and benefits, refer them to HR; that's just as much of a faux pas as not asking any questions at all.

Directly after the interview, fill in a quick rubric (see Table 16.4 for an example) to capture interview details, and score the candidate so you'll be able to compare the candidates more easily. If it's permissible, give candidates a timed writing test where they write a press release and then summarize it into an elevator pitch; for senior positions, ask candidates to draft a communication strategy. This provides insight into their critical thinking and time management skills in addition to their writing capabilities.

Table 16.4 Sample Interview Rubric

| Interviewer name: John Doe | Date interviewed: Nov. 30 | Overall score: 35 |
| Candidate name: Jane Smith | Available start date: Jan. 1 | |

Criterion	Score 5 – Outstanding 4 – Very Good 3 – Good 2 – Average 1 – Poor	Evidence	Additional Notes
Relevant subject matter experience	5	• Worked in diabetes exclusively for 5 years	
Relevant functional experience	4	• Has handled advocacy for 5 disease awareness campaigns • Has project management experience, but only on 2 disease awareness campaigns	
Project management effectiveness	4	• Seemed to have an effective editorial process to maintain quality control of deliverables	After hearing the responses, I felt like I could trust her to do the job well
Organization skills	4	• Time-blocking evangelist • Uses Gantt charts • Proficient in Microsoft Project	

(continued)

Table 16.4 (continued)

Communication skills	3	• Provided examples of being a direct, but gentle, communicator when delivering constructive critiques to team members and resolving client issues • Example about resolving conflict with her boss may indicate she becomes passive aggressive when overruled by superiors
Overall judgment	3	• Provided over-tuned strengths as her weaknesses
Team fit	3	• Sounds like she may be quickly frustrated by team members who are poor at time management
Agency culture fit	4	• She's looking for an agency where she can be split between what she knows best and a learning opportunity, even if that means putting in more hours
Asked smart questions	5	• Clearly did her homework and asked specific questions about the agency and our client list

The team leader should be the common denominator for all candidate interviews, and have a mix of peers, superiors, and less experienced staff participate. We recommend two to three additional interviews in addition to the team leader. Every interviewer should fill in a rubric following the interview. Instead of going through the same list of questions, the initial interview with the team leader can guide the focus of subsequent interviews (ie to explore cultural fit). It's then helpful to calculate each candidate's group score or average score to contribute to the decision-making process. However, the rubric is only a tool to help; clearly if someone scores high in most areas but scores low in one important area, such as a cultural fit, then they're probably not the best choice.

Team Management

Even with an ideal team mix, challenges will still arise due to the movable feast of people politics. The key to keeping the team as copasetic and effective as possible, even in times of hardship (such as under-resourcing), is to keep everyone moving toward a common goal, de-escalate and resolve issues between team members as quickly as possible, and follow all the other advice in this book to be the best professional, leader, and mentor you can be!

Every manager has their methods – you have to pick what's most important to you, make it clear to the team about what's expected, and then, most importantly, live it yourself. For example, Shalon and Kristin both cultivated a relaxed and collaborative team culture but were sticklers about work quality and client service. Provided the team followed a strict editorial process, deadlines were met, client requests were acknowledged within the business day, and all the work was on strategy and executed with precision, they weren't concerned if people came in a little late, left early, did some personal administration during the day, and so forth. Everything they demanded of their team, they demanded even more of themselves. During times of understaffing, this often meant they were the last to leave the office (often at 10 or 11 pm). Work days were consumed with meetings and calls, and the only time left to review documents was after working hours. However, it was critical to put in this extra time to ensure all work was high quality when it reached the client.

Forums for communication are also crucial for the team to function as a cohesive unit; however, team meetings can also be where time and productivity goes to die. When your team's in a time crunch on a high priority project or to produce an event, a short daily meeting for the core team is best. We recommend a 10- to 15-minute morning meeting to align responsibilities for the day, based on what was achieved the day before and how much is left to do. Standing meetings – actually standing up – can be really effective because they help everyone to stay focused and keep meetings short because standing around in one place gets uncomfortable quickly!

For most teams, it's useful to have a weekly meeting. Nonetheless, anything that can't be decided in about five minutes should be taken into a smaller forum so the rest of the team's time isn't wasted (eg issues that don't apply to the entire team, specific personal situations, etc). On very large teams, it can be helpful to have quarterly lunch meetings to provide a forum for the team to see their contribution within the bigger picture of a multi-faceted client account.

It's important to use project management software or a central document to guide the team's timeline of deliverables, and these should ladder up to the strategic execution of a project. The easiest way is to create a grid of the strategy and tactics that were signed off by the client in the communication plan, and then flesh out all the individual deliverables needed to execute each tactic. Some people prefer high-level status grids; others want granular Gantt charts. Whatever your preference, make sure it can do double-duty as the client's weekly report because otherwise you will be spending way too much time and money on account management, which irritates most clients.

Ultimately, with a few solid team management practices, you can help your team run like a well-oiled machine. New managers are often overly keen to implement multiple processes and rules that they've learned during their professional development journey. However, after almost 15 years of team management, we can honestly say that you'll have the greatest success if you put in the time and thought to get the staff mix right and then manage the team with as few rules and processes as possible.

Industry Insight

MIKE DOYLE
Partner and president, North America, Ketchum
New York, USA

Who doesn't love getting an invitation? Whether it's to a birthday party or a Broadway premiere, an invitation is a sign of inclusion. A signal that your presence will be valued and welcomed. Any great team I've built or worked with started with a series of clear, transparent, deliberate, and generous invitations.

Extend invitations based on talent and skill. When you invite someone to join your team, tell them why they're in that room, and be as specific as possible. Describe the unique skill he or she will bring to the group, and why you know the team will be better, more productive, because of their specific talent or anticipated contribution. Imagine the confidence and engagement you'll instill in your team members when they know, from the outset, exactly why they are there and what's expected of them. And as a leader, contemplate the benefits of publicly recognizing each of the team members for his or her gifts. What a gift to each of them and to the group to celebrate the reason those invitations were granted.

Extend invitations based on diversity in all its forms. Invite individuals who you know approach challenges differently than you do. Who look different than you. Who live in another town than you do, or speak a different language than you do, or have celebrated far more or far fewer birthdays than you have. Building a team with unique perspectives, ideas, and opinions – even ones that challenge your own comfort level – will result in more evolved thinking, unexpected discussion and debate, and better outcomes, because communications

(continued)

(continued)

counsel and creative are stronger when informed by human truths. You won't land on anything worth doing without over-indexing on the "human."

Extend an invitation to provide feedback – but you've got to mean it. Set the stage early for the environment you want to establish and the level of candor, humility, and honesty you expect and will give in return. Experience has taught me that teams flourish most when you create safe spaces with plenty of oxygen for others to breathe. And listen, if someone isn't comfortable with the kind of team you're creating, or doesn't feel ideally suited for the task at hand, welcome them to opt out of the experience with the same level of grace with which you extended the invitation in the first place.

When you build your next team, kick it off with the words, "Please join me . . ." or "I'd like to invite your thinking . . .". I think you'll be pleasantly surprised by the way people RSVP.

Mike is president of the North American region for Ketchum, one of the world's largest communications consultancies. He and his colleagues help companies tell their stories, connect with the people they care about most, and use communications to inspire action.

17 Personal Branding

> What you do speaks so loudly that I cannot hear what you say.
> (Ralph Waldo Emerson)

There are many great stories that teach us about ourselves but one in particular always seems to resonate with people starting their careers. It's called the "Bricklayer's Parable" and it goes something like this (embellished with some modern-day nuance):

> A woman was enjoying her weekly Friday lunchtime walk and started to approach an empty field that was near her office. It's a field she's passed nearly every Friday for the past two years, expansive and vibrant in all seasons, and she loves the calm and inspiration it offers. As she got near, she saw that the field was a bustle of activity. There were cars and trucks and loads of materials and people all looking very busy. It was not a calm field today.
>
> She walked up to a man with a hard hat on who was kneeling down, slowly working away by himself. She said, "Excuse me sir, I walk by this field every week and I'm really curious – what are you working on here?" The man stopped his labor for a moment, slowly gave a half-turn to briefly look at her, and said with no small amount of annoyance, "Lady, can't you see here I'm laying bricks. That's what's going on here."
>
> The woman backed away from the man, who was already back to work, and continued to explore the worksite taking over her beloved field. As she walked further, she saw a woman, who was also wearing a hard hat and was stooped over, working diligently on a task before her. The woman stooped over paused for a moment, and the woman on her lunchtime walk could see that this woman was also was laying bricks. Perhaps this woman could tell her what was happening, she thought. She approached the woman, "Pardon me ma'am, I walk by this field every week and I'm really curious – what are you working on here?"

The woman looked up and studied the woman in her suit and walking sneakers, with equal curiosity. "Well, after years of negotiations, they finally got the green light to put a building in this field so here we are, finally, laying some bricks for the foundation today. But this is an active construction site so you should really get back on the main road." And with that she was back to work, laying bricks, and building the foundation.

Two large dump trucks pulled in with a roar and startled the woman on her lunch break. She turned around and started making her way back to the main road. As she was walking, she encountered a man with a pile of bricks in a wheelbarrow coming toward her. Still wondering what was to become of her beloved field, she thought she'd give it one last try. "Hello, there. I walk by this field every week and I'm really curious – what are you working on here?"

The man paused, set down the loaded wheelbarrow, and took off his heavy work gloves. He wiped his brow and looked thoughtfully at the field and activity before him. The woman turned her head for a moment to look at the field too, and then back at the man again, who took a deep breath. "I've been a bricklayer for nearly 30 years," he said, as he picked up a brick from his wheelbarrow. "But today, I'm helping cure cancer. This right here is going to be a world-class cancer research facility – and I'm going to be sure it has the best foundation it can possibly have." The woman was speechless. She watched as the bricklayer gently set the brick back into the wheelbarrow, put his work gloves back on, lifted the heavy wheelbarrow, and continued on toward the worksite.

The lesson from this is that while all three bricklayers had the same role doing the same task, they each saw their work in a different light. The first saw his role as a job: he lays bricks. The second saw her role as a career: she's a bricklayer. But the third saw his role as a calling: he knew that what he did contributed to a purpose. It added value to the world in a way that was bigger than a brick or foundation on its own. He was focused on the outcome.

Being outcome focused is difficult – especially when the tasks at hand are simple tasks. *Take notes. Draft a document. Monitor media coverage.* It can be frustrating to be the one "laying the bricks" early in your career, when you know you could be the full-on architect. Yet there is merit to understanding every part of the role – and appreciating the contributions and outcome that every part of a project supports.

That's where your personal branding comes into play. We are by no means suggesting that you passively sit back and wait for a big, juicy role to come your way. However, we are encouraging – no, imploring – you to seize every opportunity that comes your way to squeeze every last drop of "calling" out of it – for you, for your boss, for your team, and for your clients. You don't need to wait for your next big presentation. Every day is a presentation! Make every moment count.

Easier said than done, of course. This is where your work is needed. "Success," according to retired champion auto racer Robert "Bobby" Unser, is defined as the meeting of preparation and opportunity (STANDS4 LLC). And, we believe preparation invites opportunity to the party.

Personal Branding in Practice

We talked in Part II about some standard technical skills you need in place to be successful in an agency, but what about some less often discussed preparation? To tighten your personal branding (or get it together in the first place), consider the following tips.

1. **You are your brand**

    In public relations (PR), your history, experience, reputation, and relationships are just as important as the technical skills that are formally required. Although people in other industries tend to compartmentalize their life – for example, "Philanthropy Kristin" and "Consultant Kristin," or "Travel Blogger Shalon" and "Executive Shalon," the worlds start to collide. First, recognize that this is inevitable in our field, and second, you need to be the one to define what that means. This means you need to find your why. Why do you do what you do, or pursue what you want to do? What difference does it make? What is the purpose?

    For example, Kristin was intent on working in healthcare communications because, like the bricklayer, she saw herself working for something from which she drew value and meaning. Maybe you find value in art, fashion, global supply chains, or start-ups . . . there's really no right or wrong way to contribute if you find it meaningful (and hopefully use your PR powers for good!).

    Once you find your brand, keep that thread tight, because that brand is not just a brand . . . that brand is you. Are you someone who cares deeply about something? Are you someone with an expertise in one sector? Are you known for specialty work, such as working with media or multicultural stakeholders in a global marketplace? The sooner you can embrace your brand, the sooner it will embrace you.

2. **Seeing is believing**

    Ninety percent of a first impression is what people see and hear from you. If you can't capture their attention, forget winning hearts and minds over with anything brilliant you have to say because, guess what, they're not listening. The good news is that capturing attention is easy. (The bad news is that keeping attention is another story for another book!) Capturing attention in a good way includes using body language, gestures, and your smile.

- *Body language*

   A strong stance – with feet planted – makes you look confident and keeps you from swaying or appearing too shifty. Open body language, with arms at the side or better yet moving, makes you look inviting and open to conversation.

- *Gestures*

   Don't be afraid to take up space. Many people only gesture from the elbow down, being careful not to make their arms reach too far or have their feet spaced too wide. Guess what? Powerful people don't apologize for taking up space – and neither should you. Arms that move are inviting and open, but the caveat is that they need to move in concert with what you're saying. If your arms are simply flailing about, you'll look odd. (We know you were thinking that too.)

- *Smile*

   Smiles are inviting, they put people at ease, and they show attentiveness. Of course, smiles are one of the trickiest impression components to master because they vary across people, situations, and cultures. Certainly, there are times when a stern face will convey that you're listening intently and a broad smile could inadvertently communicate the opposite. Our best advice, second to working with a professional presentation coach, is to study effective leaders delivering famous speeches. Notice what worked. Notice what didn't. And consider what elements you'd like to deliberately bring into your own presentation style.

3. **Nail your intro**

   Raleigh Mayer, an executive presence coach known as "The Gravitas Guru," always dismissed elevator speeches as boring. Instead, have an "inventive introduction," as she calls it. Short, pithy, and leave them wanting more. Case in point – if you met someone who said she was the Gravitas Guru, wouldn't you want to know more? So many questions come to mind! Figure out what this is for you. Who are you? What do you want to be? Get inventive. You might be saying to yourself, "I just graduated," "I just started my career," or "I don't know who I am yet." You know what we say? Excuses. There is a 110 percent chance that there is something interesting about you, but you have to believe it before anyone else will.

4. **Be consistent**

    We've said it before and we'll say it again – be consistent! Surprises can be fun, but not in business. In most professional settings, people appreciate knowing what to expect, when to expect it, and from whom. If you would like to develop an impressive personal brand, show regard for others by doing what you say you'll do each and every time. As we said in Chapter 14, promises fulfilled build trust, and this is a leadership principle you can practice no matter what your level is. If you are consistently building trust, you are most certainly supporting your personal brand.

5. **Be outstanding**

    In fact, be consistently outstanding. Consistently wow people. This may be the exception of where surprises are good in the professional setting – because people will be surprised by anyone who consistently surpasses expectations. The reward for good work is more work, so see that for what it is – a reward. More responsibility – be it in the form of meatier work, more access, or even a bigger role (read: title + money!) – means more trust in you and recognition for your efforts. Bravo! There's nothing but advancement if you're consistently outstanding.

Personal branding will happen with or without you. If you choose to manage your brand, you'll be in the seat of power. However, if you fail to define your brand, we guarantee others will do it for you and you may not like the results. Therefore, go the extra mile and you'll get ahead by a marathon. Fast track it. It's not easy, but it's certainly worth it. And if you lose sight of your why, see Tip 1.

References

Mayer, Raleigh. *Raleigh Mayer: Gravitas Guru*, www.gravitasguru.info.

STANDS4 LLC. "Bobby Unser Quotes." *Quotes.net*, STANDS4 LLC, 4 Oct. 2018, www.quotes.net/quote/18473.

Industry Insight

KEN KERRIGAN, APR

Executive vice president, Weber Shandwick
New York, USA

I'll never forget my first performance review. It was 1989 and I was six months into my first job at a small PR agency in New York City. I thought a raise might be coming my way or, at the very least, I'd be hearing about what a great job I was doing. I was wrong on both counts. Here's what the chief executive officer (CEO) of the agency (we'll call him "Bob") had to say to me in my review, "Ken, you're a fraud and a failure, and I think you'll be found out at any agency you go to large or small." I honestly don't remember how I responded. I like to think I laughed (I know I didn't tear up), but I think I was more likely stunned into silence.

What people say about you, especially in things like performance reviews, can define who you are and, maybe more importantly, how you are seen by others. What sticks depends on how you respond.

I'm happy to report that I was able to leave the agency a few weeks after this review for a job at a competing firm for substantially more money. When the time came to walk out the door, just for spite, I took the only key to the men's room and put it in my pocket. I still have it. However, I'd be lying if I said I didn't take this first review seriously, because I still think about it 30 years later.

You can let a negative comment define you or you can let it drive you forward. I chose the latter. In doing so, whether unconsciously or not, I began to develop a "challenger" brand for myself. As part of this personal brand, I accepted that my career wasn't going to be handed to me on a silver platter. I'd need to work harder, push myself to stay ahead of what's next in the industry, and never be satisfied with status quo ideas.

This branding approach, even if only viewed internally, has served me well. I have gone on to work for some of the most respected companies in the world and I've held senior positions at the largest agencies. Looking back, that performance review was probably the best thing that's happened to me in my career. I don't think that's what "Bob" intended, but then again, his agency no longer exists and I'm still here and nowhere near done.

Ken has been practicing PR for more than 30 years. He wanted to go to law school but they wouldn't let him in so he decided to argue in the court of public opinion instead. He lives and works in New York City.

18 Managing Your Career

> If you think you can do a thing or think you can't do a thing, you're right.
> (Henry Ford)

Earlier in this book (see Chapter 4), we focused a lot on the "vertical" – the proverbial corporate ladder – for the sake of explaining billing. Now we're talking about managing your career and we have three words for you: forget the ladder. We're borrowing this idea from Sheryl Sandberg who borrowed it from *Fortune* magazine editor Pattie Sellers, who brilliantly describes her successful career climb not up a ladder, but rather on a jungle gym. In her book *Lean In: Women, Work, and the Will to Lead*, she describes how the jungle gym offers many ways to the top, with creative twists, turns, dips, detours and even some dead ends (Yarow).

Embracing the idea of a creative jungle gym-esque approach to your career is helpful because the truth is, there is no single road to the top. Every person makes his or her own path. It's normal in your career to be fearful – okay, terrified – of making a mistake or the wrong choice. Yet fear of failure doesn't do anything but hold you back from moving forward. What some people call failure, we call lessons, and if you're learning, then you're growing, and you're somewhere further along than where you started. Hey – you're already making strides by reading this book!

If you want to work in a public relations (PR) agency, your career trajectory is entirely in your hands. If you're lucky, you may find a mentor or have a good manager who might assign activities to develop your skills and promote you – but that would be a bonus. For the most part, it's on you to set your goals, achieve them, and advocate for appropriate recognition, whether that be new responsibilities, a promotion, a raise, all of the above, and/or more. Of course, it doesn't all work that smoothly or quickly. Inevitably, there are mistakes along the way. The only way to get through mistakes is with humility: take responsibility for your mistakes; learn from them; and figure out how to ensure they won't happen again. For people who are new in their careers, this "advancement process," if we can call it that, is sometimes a bit of a surprise. However, it's a good surprise and to your advantage if you have the appetite to strive to deliver excellent work (and own up when you occasionally mess up).

Think about it from the client's perspective: in agencies, clients who are billed by the hour are getting charged in 15-minute increments. That adds up! It's incredibly important that whoever is working on behalf of the client has solid skills and the capacity to consistently deliver excellent work. Therefore, agencies typically don't promote someone until they are already doing the work of the next level. "Good enough" is not good enough in client service. And for the clients' sake, that's reasonable. To advance your career, its critical to hone your skills, gain experience, expand your contributions, and deliver excellence consistently.

Advancement in Three Steps

When it comes to managing your career, goals are essential. While there are no shortcuts to offer, there are three steps to guide you to better position yourself to move forward faster: define; focus; and grow.

1. **Define**

    You've likely heard from someone along the way that "you can do anything." Perhaps that's true. But "anything" doesn't mean "everything at the same time." So pick something. Choose one to three specific professional goals to tackle at this moment. For example, maybe you want to work at a PR agency. Excellent! Yet there are literally hundreds of agencies to choose from in multiple geographies doing a ton of different things. You could waste years hopping from one agency to the next until you find a good fit – or you could pursue something that excites you from the beginning.

    A more directive way to approach goal setting is to use the SMART goals model. George T Doran published this goal setting approach in the journal *Management Review* in 1981 and, to this day, it's an approach everyone from PR agencies to blue-chip corporations use for mapping out ambitions. SMART goals, as you might guess, is an acronym for this mapping process. As you're setting your goals, ask yourself if they are the following.

    - *Specific:* The fastest way to move toward your goal is to define what it is. Do you want to work at a big, medium, or small agency? Do you want to be in any particular region or city? Will it be a public or private agency? Do you prefer to work in a specific sector, such as consumer or technology? Do you have a specific functional role you want to pursue, such as a media relations expert or a multicultural expert? The more specific you can be with your goals, the more likely it is you'll enjoy not only the "destination," but the pursuit.
    - *Measurable:* How do you know when you've reached your goal? You need some way to evaluate your success. You define this for yourself. Is it when you "get a job"? That doesn't seem very

specific. How about when you get an agency role in New York as a senior account executive (SAE) working for entertainment sector clients"? Warmer? What about "when you land a vice president position at an agency doing PR for Beyoncé"? Now we're talking!

- ***Achievable***: Okay, now let's consider if what you've specified and how you'll know when you've reached your goal – measurement – are achievable. The Beyoncé goal gets points for ambition, but perhaps we can scale for more immediate success. We're not going to deride anyone's dreams, but it is advisable to have small steps in place on the way to reaching your larger goals. Specify your goal so that it's a challenge, but within reach. Perhaps working in an agency role in New York at the SAE level for entertainment sector clients, with a 15 percent salary increase, is a good way to kick things off on your road to representing an entertainment and cultural icon like Beyoncé.
- ***Realistic***: Ask yourself if what you're doing is in line with achieving your goal. Is it worth your time in order to have the outcome you want? What are you going to actually achieve given your resources? There are a lot of distractions that will tempt you away from your goals, but if something isn't realistic and driving you closer to your intended results, then re-evaluate. Keeping with our entertainment PR example, if this is truly your goal, don't give in when a recruiter calls with a role in a completely different industry, doing non-PR work, with a lucrative salary. Pursue what will get you to your goal.
- ***Time-bound***: Give yourself a timeline and hold yourself accountable. Block out time in your calendar if you have to or enlist an "accountability" buddy to help you stick with your timeline. As the saying goes, "if nothing changes, nothing changes."

2. **Focus**

Once you've defined your SMART goals, pursue them with laser focus. Let nothing deter you from getting to your goal. (The one exception we'll make is if something even more amazing, aligned with your goal, comes along while in hot pursuit of your specific goal. As discussed in Chapter 17, we like to call that, "opportunity.")

Pursuing your goals with focus can be broken down into three stages: study; sweat; and crush it.

In the "study" stage, you become the expert. Research. Theoretically, ask "What is there to know about your goal?" If you'd like to work for a specific agency, for example, learn everything you can about that agency. Who are the clients? What specialties does the agency offer? What are the backgrounds of leaders who work there, and what can you learn from their experience?

If you're already working in an agency and would like to get promoted or recognized for new projects, pay attention to colleagues and leaders who you admire. What is it that makes them successful? How do they manage their time? How do they manage personal relationships? You'll probably find that they're efficient yet precise, candid yet considerate, and laidback yet professional. Depending on your team, your client, and your own personal style, you'll need to determine the right balance of these things and more. This means also taking an honest inventory of your own strengths and weaknesses – and adjusting accordingly. The important thing is that you have a conscious awareness of what these subtle success traits are so that you can integrate them into your own personal development and work.

In the "sweat" stage, your focus is put to the test. You may encounter uncertainty or discomfort, but you cannot let temporary hurdles shatter your dreams. If you want to work for a specific agency, for example, it may mean turning down offers from other agencies and taking a temp job to get by while interviewing for not one, not two, but three different jobs at your dream PR agency until you land a plum role. (True story.) Or if you've been working early and late for months on end because your client is in crisis, stick with it and embrace the experience as an opportunity. (Again, true story.) And, if supervisors are telling you that your work needs improvement, really consider the gift of that feedback – and it is a gift. It will make you better. (Yep – true story.) In essence, if your goal is worth pursuing, then power through adversity by continuously learning and growing, and make it happen.

In addition to embracing the stumbles and growing pains, capture your successes. You will get emails from colleagues, managers, and even clients who will thank you for your contribution or compliment your work. File that! Kudos, bravos, praise, clap back, warm fuzzies – whatever you want to name this folder – it will become a resource for you when you're trying to establish the case for your hire or promotion (and it will give you a much-needed emotional boost on hard days).

Finally, in the "crush it" stage, don't just settle for achieving your goal – crush it. Part of fulfilling your promise to yourself is taking whatever you've worked to achieve and doing all you can to be your best – dare we say, *the* best – at it. So, as an example, if your goal is to work at a specific PR agency and you've done your homework and secured the job, be consistently great at it. Show up early. Raise your hand for new assignments. Support your team. Be honest. Be kind. Listen, learn, and keep moving forward.

3. **Grow**

    Finally, once you've specified your goals and pursued them with focus, give yourself a pat on the back, get a sip of water (or wine!), and then get back out there. Because guess what? It's time to set new goals and keep growing. Never stop. At the point when you're setting new goals, you are in many ways already a new version of yourself. You've perhaps faced doubt, fear, and the mild discomfort of self-discipline, all to enjoy the sweet success of achieving something you set out to do. Growth is not only moving forward, however; it's also about looking back and appreciating where you came from and the lessons – sometimes masked as "failures," – along the way.

Your career is uniquely yours. A wise mentor, author, professor, coach, and business owner – Helio Fred Garcia – once said to Kristin that if you think of your career as a Venn diagram, "you can do what you love, you can do what you're good at, or you can do what people will pay you to do." Ideally, you'll eventually accomplish all three at the same time. While working toward that, specify, focus, and grow to move forward faster.

References

Doran, G. T. "There's a S.M.A.R.T. Way to Write Management's Goals and Objectives." *Management Review*, vol. 70, no. 11, 1981, pp. 35–36.

Yarow, Jay. "Sheryl Sandberg's Full HBS Speech: Get on a Rocketship Whenever You Get the Chance." *Business Insider*, 25 May 2012, www.businessinsider.com/sheryl-sandbergs-full-hbs-speech-get-on-a-rocketship-whenever-you-get-the-chance-2012-5.

Industry Insight

ALANA ROCKLAND

Group director earned media, W2O Group
New York, USA

To this day, I still remember the pride I felt from my first media placement. It was for a beauty line on a website called Afrobella. Even though it was just a couple of sentences about a new shampoo, the thrill of success, albeit a small one, stayed with me. From that point on, I was hooked on media relations – there is nothing like being able to hold up a magazine article or watch the news on television, knowing I worked with a reporter to bring that story to life.

However, I spent my first two agency jobs paying my dues (developing call agendas, taking notes, logistical planning, etc). The people around me weren't particularly encouraging or supportive of my interest in specializing in media relations – my managers wanted me to become part of the core account team despite my natural aptitude and interest in media relations. I kept raising my hand to work on media activities across my accounts, which helped me to develop relationships with top health reporters and carve out a niche as a media specialist.

Today, I'm a group director at a top marketing communications firm leading media relations for large, cutting-edge healthcare companies, and working with influential outlets such as *The Today Show, Good Morning America, CNN*, and *USA Today*. My approach to relationship building is what's helped me to get my dream job – my relationships with reporters are my priority, so when working with the media, I selectively pitch story ideas to reporters based on what will interest them. It

(continued)

(continued)

is important to spend the time getting to know each reporter to ensure I make their job easier by giving them only news they will want.

Remember, your career is long and will have ups and downs, so it's important to find something you are truly passionate about. For me, it will always be healthcare media relations, for you it may be another functional specialty like digital or new business development or a specific sector like consumer products or technology. The key is to figure out what your passion is and then to keep volunteering to do work that you love to build your expertise, even if it's above and beyond your assigned workload.

Alana is a senior media relations expert specializing in healthcare and disease awareness programs. Her expertise lies in fostering relationships with top-tier media.

19 Managing the Careers of Others

> We make a living by what we get, but we make a life by what we give.
>
> (Unknown)

When you get to the point in your career where people are answering to you, congratulations! You're a manager! However, this means you have both your job and the responsibility for someone else's career growth, to a degree. Whether you've had good mentors and managers or whether you've suffered poor mentors and managers, we all know that helping people is the right thing to do.

Managers have a responsibility to their staff to oversee not only the work that gets done, and on a larger scale the client relationships, but also the career of those contributing to the manager's team. Of course, while personal career growth is truly up to the individual, a good manager will look out for their junior team members to ensure they have a healthy balance. This means assigning ample work, but not too much. It also means providing work that is challenging, but within one's ability. And it also means considering where junior team members will thrive, learn, and grow.

The Gift of Managing

Great managers take this responsibility to heart and are never forgotten by their protégés. Generosity as a manager comes with a price, however. If you're working at an agency and managing a team, time is money. Any extra time you spend with a junior team member speaking about career, skillsets, or development topics is time that you are not billing to client work. There are a set number of hours to fulfill with billable client work, nonetheless. Therefore, taking time out to mentor truly is giving a gift of your time, experience, and wisdom.

Like all the best gifts, the giver also becomes the recipient. Taking time to invest in developing your people may, initially, seem like a gamble. You could nurture someone's talent only to see them leave the company once they become high performers. Or you could develop someone and they could go on to be your star team member. Regardless, scratch the word "gamble" from this equation. If you've made it to manager, you're someone who sets goals, specifies what they are, sweats to achieve them, and re-evaluates success for continued achievement and growth. That same approach can be applied to managing the careers of others.

If you are teaching, and if you are guiding, then you are moving people forward. Though it's to the company's benefit to keep employees at the company and teams intact, the most well-functioning teams are those in which people are treated well and are genuinely happy to be there. You don't want people on your team who don't want to be there. So, invest to a fault in the people you manage and know that it's worth it. It's elective, but it makes a better team that typically provides better work to clients. Plus, you never know – someone you manage may leave your team for an in-house role, only to come back and hire you and your agency team for the mere fact that they know you do excellent work, are committed to doing the right thing, and that you care.

Become an Exceptional Manager

As you grow in your public relations (PR) agency career, you'll quickly take stock of what "not" to do. Examples of bad managers are unfortunately abundant. Partly because, in general, managing others is hard and therefore often done poorly, and partly because it's human nature to complain, and in agencies we work in teams, so it's likely we hear more about the "bad ones." In fact, there's a common saying that "People never leave jobs, they leave managers." And certainly, you don't want people to leave! What about the good, great, and exceptional managers? They are absolutely out there as well. If you want to be an exceptional manager, consider the five tips for leadership below. Much of it is what we have touched on already in Part IV, so this should start to sound familiar to you.

- ***Set expectations***

    Ground rules are important for giving people a target. What is the work product that you expect from the people you manage? What behavior and culture are appropriate for your team, and even for client interactions? What should people expect if they decide to "do their own thing"? Remember that you're a manager: you may have to adjust some relationships to ensure clarity of roles for the benefit of all, but objectively upholding the expectations you set will go a long way in creating harmony and achievement on your team.

- *Lead by example*

    We know we've beat on this drum a lot, but it's one of the most critical pieces of advice we can impart. "Do as I say, not as I do" is out. Teams will look to you for what's acceptable, and calibrate their contributions to what they observe from you. If you want your team to be open, collaborative, and diligent, for example, then that's exactly how you need to work with them.

- *Provide honest feedback*

    In client service, even though exceptional work is what's expected, praise does play a critical role. Recognition makes people feel valuable and appreciated, which makes them want to work harder and never let you down. And guess what? Sending an email recognizing a job well done and copying in your boss and your boss's boss is free, so there's no need to be stingy. With that said, you also want your praise to truly mean something so don't dole it out unless it is truly deserved. Conversely, honestly address issues objectively and immediately if they arise. For new managers, it's sometimes difficult to talk to others about improvement, but you are doing no one any favors by permitting sub-par work or inappropriate behavior. Ignoring problems fails to support the development of an underperforming professional at best, and at worst can bring down team morale or a client relationship. Be honest, objective, and timely with your feedback.

- *Delegate and let go*

    Part of managing means just that: you manage! Assemble a team that you trust has the skills to do the jobs that have to be done and then allow them to do those jobs. Be available and supportive so that the team knows they have access to you and can come to you with any hint of issues – but allow them to do the work. Trust – trust in yourself that you've allocated the right work to the right people, and trust that those people will rise to the occasion. This not only helps your team members to develop their skills and contributions, but it frees you up to do other more account management focused tasks. Delegating and letting go creates a balanced team that produces excellent work.

- *Stay humble*

    Recall from Chapter 18 that we should all be in a place of setting new goals and growing. It doesn't matter if you're a chief executive officer (CEO) – there is always more to do and more to be. When you are a manager, it's important to maintain a sense of humility. PR, at its core, is about relationships. Humility inspires your team to follow you because they want to follow you.

While the example you set is critical, how you mentor carries just as much weight. It's a daunting task to figure out your own path let alone the paths of others. One of the most helpful tools we've encountered is performance company Forty2's coaching conversation construct, which explores the past, evaluates the present, and plans for the future. Our take on this is as follows.

- *Explore the past*

    Ask open-ended questions (that can't be answered with a "yes" or a "no") to see what the team member has achieved or thinks has gone well. From there, you can provide positive feedback and any specific thoughts about their achievements and past performance.

- *Evaluate the present*

    Once again, open-ended questions are key to get your team members to open up to you. Inquire about strengths, which parts of their job they feel passionate about, and any areas they would like to improve. Do not interrupt – it's essential during these conversations that you truly listen. Only after there's a long pause, and it's clear they are finished, can you add your perspective for consideration.

- *Plan for the future*

    This is the most important part – where you ascertain what someone's ambitions are, what gets them out of bed in the morning, and how they think they can leverage their strengths to achieve their dreams. Not to sound like a broken record, but make sure all the questions you ask are open-ended and get specific – down to the actions this person needs to take in the next quarter to make strides toward fulfilling their career aspirations. After the conversation, the team member should memorialize the plan in writing, including any training required, and submit it to you for review. Make sure the goals are SMART and the steps to achieve the goals are clear.

Making the plan is critical so that you have a baseline for regular future discussions and to measure progress. Whether your PR agency has a formal development process or not, you should help your team members to make performance plans – it will help them to achieve their goals and, in turn, they will give you their best.

Reference

Forty2. "Coaching Conversation." Leadership seminars, Coaching Conversation, 2015.

Industry Insight

ABBIE GRIFFITH

Executive vice president, Edelman
New York, USA

Almost two decades ago when I entered the industry, my very first boss took a chance on me, a bright-eyed, hopeful, ambitious college grad with a curiosity about PR and an insatiable desire to know what working in PR was all about. The first firm I joined was a mid-sized agency that moved at an incredibly fast pace, which was easy to get swallowed up in – but my boss always took the extra step to make sure I was clear on the task at hand, whether it was his copy-edits to a press release I had written, details on a meeting that needed to be quickly coordinated, or any number of other responsibilities. He was generous with his time and, most importantly, led by example. I decided if I was ever a manager, my philosophy in terms of people management would be to make my teams feel as valued as he made me feel, leading to greater productivity and higher job satisfaction.

Now, as an executive vice president of a 100+ person practice at a global PR firm, I am responsible for the careers of many others – but my philosophy on being an exceptional manager hasn't changed. Quite simply, it's based on doing what's necessary to bring out the best in the people that I'm responsible for. At the end of the day, if your teams are inspired, motivated, fulfilled, and equipped with the confidence and skills to do an excellent job on behalf of your clients, then you are doing your job.

A big part of ensuring this happens is making the choice to invest in your people. Whether that's meeting before work, taking the time to coach them on an assignment, encouraging them to take

(continued)

(continued)

on stretch assignments, or just making the time to get to know your team beyond the client work, it's the effort that you make to bond with your team that will matter the most. I have always found that my teams respond best when they know that they have a manager who is committed to being an ally and an advocate.

I'm not going to pretend that being an impactful manager or mentor in our industry is easy. The days can be oh so long in the world of PR, with the constant pressure of deadlines, client asks, deliverables, new business pitches, to name just a few. The truth is it can be hard to make time for yourself, much less the individuals on your team. However, I firmly believe that investing time, energy, and mentorship in the colleagues that you manage is one of the most rewarding actions that you take as a PR professional.

Abbie is an executive vice president at Edelman, the world's largest, independently-owned PR firm. She oversees a team of more than 100 PR professionals to provide exemplary client service, relationship building, effective organizational infrastructure, culture, and talent development. She has over 15 years of experience servicing Fortune 500 clients and spanning the communications marketing spectrum, including earned media, consumer engagement, digital communications, celebrity and experiential activations, employee engagement, data/brand milestone management, and pharmaceutical regulatory approvals at the local, regional, and global level.

20 Managing Client Relationships

> Life is 10% what happens to me and 90% how I react to it.
> (Charles R. Swindoll)

If you can manage expectations then you have most of what you need to manage client relationships successfully. The rest comes down to building rapport, acting with integrity, and demonstrating commitment. Establishing solid client relationships is crucial to any business but especially to consulting businesses like public relations (PR), where a single client relationship can often compose a significant chunk of an agency's revenue.

Building Rapport

This is where the road becomes difficult – you know the client is the hand that feeds you, your team, and your agency, so the natural instinct is to make the client happy at all costs. The pressure is likely to challenge your ability to remain authentic because instinct will encourage you to act submissively to preserve the relationship. However, this will have the opposite of the desired effect. As we discussed in Chapter 12, clients trust authentic consultants and trust, which is the product of expectations fulfilled, combined with clear communication is the foundation of rapport.

Cast your mind back to a time when you felt like an acquaintance was complimenting you non-stop, disconcertingly agreeable, and catering to you. Maybe there was a situation where you were popular in school and someone was trying to curry favor, or a colleague wanted you to ease the burden of their workload. Did they seem disingenuous? Did you trust that person? Would you take advice from someone like that? Would you want to spend any length of time with that person? The answer is probably "no."

Now, think about people in your life that you trust and have rapport with – parents, siblings, best friends, teachers, mentors, and classmates might spring to mind. Why do you trust these people over the robots? It's most likely because you think these people have your back – they celebrate your wins, are sympathetic to your losses, and through it all they give you honest advice when you ask for it.

The key to cultivating rapport with your clients is to build trust by setting and fulfilling realistic expectations, being authentic in all of your interactions, and providing good counsel when asked (or when you ask permission to provide an opinion). Kicking it off could be a simple as coordinating a meet-and-greet. Find out what the client values and how the client works. Is this a client who prefers phone calls or are they okay with email? Does the client like regular updates or prefer you and your agency team to run with it and check in as needed? What about counsel? Does this client want to know every idea that comes to your mind? Or, similar to personal relationships, does unsolicited advice agitate? Even though the client is technically paying you to provide advice, it's still a good rule of thumb to always ask them before serenading them with your opinions – no matter how experienced you are.

Acting with Integrity

Integrity should already be one of the values you identified in Chapter 12. If it's not, know that if you do not act with integrity in your professional life, it will come back to haunt you, probably at the worst possible moment. With that said, you should act with integrity because you want to, not because you have to (it will come off as disingenuous anyway).

Here's the rub, in PR there are a lot of gray areas as to what "doing the right thing" looks like. The best thing for you to do is to act in accordance with your values, your agency's values, the values of your client's company, and the values of the PR industry, as defined by the Public Relations Society of America (PRSA). When in doubt, do not act at all – seek counsel. There will inevitably come a point in your career when a client asks you to do something and your gut will tell you it's wrong, but because it's for *the client*, you feel like you should probably give in and do it anyway. No matter how much experience you have or what your role is, you should not do anything that you perceive to be wrong or that makes you feel uncomfortable.

Here are a few examples of sticky client requests that you may face.

- Omitting information required by law to be disclosed in a press release.
- Cherry-picking data in a press release.
- Cherry-picking sources of information for external communications.
- Lacking transparency on social media.
- Not disclosing funding sources.
- Not disclosing relationships that conflict with the client.
- Posing as someone else to conduct competitive reconnaissance.

Ultimately, the client is going to respect you more if you decline to do something morally or legally questionable. With that said, the rule still holds that you should never say "no" – try to help the client see that going about whatever it is a different way will be more beneficial to them, their company's reputation, and their outcome. As consultants, we can only offer counsel (we can't force anyone's hand); there is a chance of being overruled, which means the account lead will have to resolve the situation with the client. If the account lead gives in and asks you to do whatever it is anyway, you do not have to agree. Just because you're told to do something does not mean that you will not be held accountable for your actions later by the client's company, your agency, and the law (depending on what it is).

Some clients are new themselves and aren't even aware that what they're asking for isn't completely okay, so you will earn their respect and trust if you flag that "X" request could be perceived as a violation of "Y" regulation and that it may be best to take "Z" approach instead.

Part of acting with integrity is not getting up on your high horse or moral soapbox and looking down on others, but rather gently doing the right thing and helping others to do the same without shaming them in the process. Acting with integrity also means owning your errors, never passing blame on to others, and not making excuses (although if you follow the advice in Chapter 14 on managing expectations, you'll never have to).

Demonstrating Commitment

Whether you're really excited about a client's account or not, you need to be genuinely committed to doing the best you possibly can for that client. While natural enthusiasm is likely to help expedite building rapport, being committed to the client long term is the statement that really matters.

Quality of thought and work is the most important thing you can do to demonstrate commitment. If you put in the time to know the client's business inside out, you'll be able to be strategic, tactical, and/or thoughtful with the work whether it's providing strategic counsel or editing a document. Also, make sure everything you deliver to the client is proofed, data checked, and aligned with their branding guidance in tone, language, and design. Even if you do all the big things right, the little things can quickly undermine a previously harmonious relationship.

In addition to delivering consistent quality, bend over backward to help your clients – answer urgent calls after hours, invest in teaching them or their department a skill (eg social media), or stay with them for the long haul when an event goes long. If they feel like you're in the trenches with them, they will feel like you are committed to their account and, ideally, an integral part of their team.

Make your client feel special – like they're the only one, even though they know they're not. They know you're juggling clients, but don't rub it in their face. They're spending a lot of money with your agency and want to know they have your attention. Move internal meetings/deadlines to better accommodate client meeting/deadline requests; don't talk about your other current clients unless asked or there's a learning that would directly benefit this client (and you're allowed to share); and don't use your other clients as an excuse for not delivering quality work on time.

In conclusion, client relationships can take a lot of time and energy to build, but without the personal bond, you're just a vendor and your work is simply a transaction. Building rapport, doing the right thing, and demonstrating commitment will create a halo effect around you, your team, and your agency. This aura of positivity will help you retain the client long term, organically grow the business, and encourage clients to forgive an occasional mistake or misunderstanding that may happen along the way.

Industry Insight

KATARINA NILSSON

Global portfolio communications lead, top 10 global pharmaceutical company
Sweden and Denmark

When I left the agency world in New York City to go in-house at a big pharma company in Europe, I brought over a decade of experience and felt that I had a pretty good understanding of what to expect. How different could it be "on the other side"? Well, as it turns out, very different.

During my agency years, I sometimes found myself frustrated with the lack of response from clients. This was especially true between 10 am and 3 pm, after which point client email responses started to flood my inbox. Little did I know that my clients were most likely stuck in back-to-back meetings most of the day. And when I say meetings, I mean the kind of meetings where you leave with a number of new actions and projects to discuss, align, plan, develop, and execute.

If there is one thing that your clients do not have, it is time. It doesn't matter how many times you send the same email reminder to your client – they are not responding because they simply can't find the time to do so. These days, I often tell my agency that "90 percent of what I do is stakeholder management." That is not an exaggeration. That is simply what a day looks like on "the other side."

So how can I help you build good relationships with your clients? Well, I have thought of a few simple tricks that I know would help tremendously:

(continued)

(continued)

- Instead of writing long feature emails, pick up the phone and call.
- If you have an email trail going back and forth, update the subject line with every response so the client knows what the action is and what is being sent.
- Create an agency email so the client only needs to track one sender. We receive multiple emails during the day and can't keep track of who sent what from the agency team.
- Weekly calls: keep them short, efficient, and focused on priority items. A client most likely doesn't need an hour with the whole agency team every week.
- Time is the only thing your client does not have, so manage it carefully.

Last but not least is one of my pet peeves: always proof your communication before sending it to the client. It is always better to spend an extra hour proofing to make sure that what you send is perfect. If not, the client will always feel the need to proof everything you send before sharing it with stakeholders.

I hope you find these simple tricks helpful. Clients are not monsters; we are simply trying to fit a lot of things into an already full calendar.

Katarina spent over a decade working at multiple PR agencies in New York City. She brought her deep knowledge and understanding of healthcare PR into the pharmaceutical industry when she joined a global top 10 pharmaceutical company in Europe. Now she resides in Sweden with her husband and two daughters.

Part V
Pay It Forward

21 A Message from the Authors

> When you learn, teach. When you get, give.
>
> (Maya Angelou)

We wish that there had been a book like this available to us when we entered agency life. After comparing our individual public relations (PR) agency experiences in hindsight, we learned that we both went into our agency careers with the assumption and confidence that we could jump right in and get to work. We were naïve. There was nothing in our education, past work experience, or technical capability that would sufficiently prepare us for the complexity and demands that PR agency life entails. It took years of successes and failures, big and small, for us to truly get it. And it took many more years to have the perspective to appreciate that insight, capture it, and share it with you today.

Despite the challenges and pressures that are inevitable in client service work such as a PR agency, the work that happens day in and day out is downright inspiring. There is an understanding – not a hope or a wish, but a true conviction – that every day everyone in the agency can be more and do more. Expectations are high. Perfection isn't applauded. Mistakes can be devastating. But the outcomes are extraordinary. If you work in a PR agency, there will be days of your life that you look back on and ask, "How did I do that?"

When that awe-struck moment inevitably hits you, remind yourself that it was you and your team that did great things – never you alone. Contrary to what some might think, clients are not the core of a PR agency. PR agencies, at their very core, are about teams. Nothing is accomplished in an agency without the coordinated efforts of many talented people working together to achieve a shared goal.

That spirit of teamwork never left us, nor has the deep conviction that when any individual enhances their skills, everyone benefits. Therefore, we offer this book as our packaged experience in the hope that it will be helpful to anyone who could benefit from a little hard-knocks PR agency wisdom.

It's personal yet representative, and candid though not comprehensive. We couldn't possibly prepare you for every situation in every agency with every team for every client. Yet the tips and tools within will help you to be a stronger team member, advisor, and leader – all important roles to master on your journey to grow your career and become an indispensable leader in PR. We wish you the best!

Contributors

Chapter 4	Mike Kuczkowski, chief executive officer (CEO), Orangefiery
Chapter 5	Thea Linscott, vice president of business development, MSL
Chapter 6	Chen Liang, consultant, Ruder Finn Asia
Chapter 7	Banks Willis, senior vice president, Spectrum Communications
Chapter 8	Meredith Topalanchik, senior vice president, G&S Business Communications
Chapter 9	Michael Estevez, managing director, Public Affairs and Crisis Communications, Burson Cohn & Wolfe
Chapter 10	Kristin Engdahl Zipay, vice president, Edelman
Chapter 11	Conroy Boxhill, managing director, Porter Novelli
Chapter 12	Veronica Marshall, creative instigator and purveyor of imagination
Chapter 13	Jeff Maldonado, managing director, KWT Global
Chapter 14	Ali Gee, senior partner and deputy CEO, FleishmanHillard Fishburn
Chapter 15	Brian N. Lee, APR, president, Revelation PR, Advertising & Social Media
Chapter 16	Mike Doyle, partner and president, North America, Ketchum
Chapter 17	Ken Kerrigan, APR, executive vice president, Weber Shandwick
Chapter 18	Alana Rockland, group director earned media, W2O Group
Chapter 19	Abbie Griffith, executive vice president, Edelman
Chapter 20	Katarina Nilsson, global portfolio communications lead, top 10 global pharmaceutical company

Index

Page numbers in *italics* refer to figures. Page numbers in **bold** refer to tables.

account directors 13, 46
account managers 13, 46
account team structure 13
achievable goals 122
activity reports 34
adaptation 68
advancement process 120
advocacy 54
agency basics: architecture of agency life 9–15; budget basics 37–44; business life cycle 16–28; ethical conduct 53–57; money basics 29–36; overview of 7; staffing 45–52; writing essentials 58–63
agency ecosystem 9
agency structure 9–12
American Tobacco Company 93
Angelou, Maya 141
annual billing power 48–50, **49**
architecture of agency life 9–15
assertiveness 74
attention, capturing 115–116
authenticity 61, 72–77, 133

Bernays, Edward L. 54, 92–93
billing code system 41
billing models 32–34, **33**
billing rates *11*
billing the client 31–32
Bloomberg, Michael 59
body language 116
Boxhill, Conroy 70–71
"Bricklayer's Parable" 113–114
budget basics 37–44, 31, **40**, **103**
business life cycle 16–28
business structure, importance of understanding 5
business development (biz dev) 16

capacity plan 50
career management 120–124, 127–130
caring 94
"CEO Genome Project" (*Harvard Business Review*) 67–69
Churchill, Winston 29
citations 59–60
client relationships 133–136
cold-calling 17
commitment, demonstrating 135–136
composure 68
confidentiality 55, 59
consensus building 89
consideration 81
consistency 95, 117
content, finalizing 60
contracts 29–30, 38
contributions 94–95
"crush it" stage 123
Crystallizing Public Opinion (Bernays) 92

data check 59–60
day-to-day work **12**
decisiveness 67–68
declining projects 26
define 121–122
delegating 129
deliverables 31, 59–60
diplomacy 80–83
disappointment 86, 89
disclosure of non-public information 55
Doran, George T. 121
Doyle, Mike 111–112

Einstein, Albert 92
Eisenhower, Dwight D. 80
email 59, 60–61
Emerson, Ralph Waldo 113

Index   145

emotional intelligence 75–76
Emotional Intelligence 2.0 (Bradberry et al.) 75, 76
engagement 68
Engdahl Zipay, Kristin 62–63
"engineering of consent" 54–55, 92
Estevez, Michael 56–57
ethical conduct 53–57, 134–135
expectations: managing 86–89; setting 128
expertise 54

fairness 54
favors, earning 82–83
fear, letting go of 73
feedback, providing honest 129
Fey, Tina 101
financial management 29–36
flat organizational structure 9–12, *11*, **12**, 37
flat project billing rate 31–34, **33**
focus 122–123
Franklin, Benjamin 5
fraud 55
freelancers 50
Freud, Sigmund 92

Garcia, Helio Fred 124
Gates, Bill 4
Gee, Ali 90–91
gestures 116
goals 73, 121–122, 130
Griffith, Abbie 131–132
growth 25–26, 124

Half, Robert 45
hierarchical organizational structure 9–12, *11*, **12**, 37–42
hiring 104–108
holding companies **10**
honesty 54, 80
hourly fee billing 31–34, **33**, 37–42, *39*
humility 129
Hunt, Bertha 93

independence 54
indispensability 5
industry awards 17
inner critic 73
insider trading 55
integrity, acting with 134–135
interest, showing genuine 74
interviewing 105–108, *107–108*
"inventive introduction" 116
invoicing 32–34, 37

jungle gym metaphor 120
junior staff 13, 46

Kerrigan, Ken 118–119
Kipling, Rudyard 58
Kuczkowski, Mike 14–15

leadership: authenticity and 72–77; behaviors demonstrating 67–69; career management and 120–124, 127–130; client relationships and 133–136; diplomacy and persuasion and 80–83; managing expectations and 86–89; in middle management 99; overview of 65; personal branding and 113–117; personal relationships and 92–96; team building and 101–110; tips for 128–130
leading by example 67, 129
Lean In (Sandberg) 120
Lee, Brian N. 97
legal issues 29–30
letter-of-agreement (LOA) 30
Liang, Chen 35–36
Linscott, Thea 27–28
listening 80–81
Lombardi, Vince 16
loyalty 54

Maldonado, Jeff 84–85
managing others 127–130
Marshall, Veronica 78–79
master services agreement 30
Mayer, Raleigh 116
measurable goals 121–122
media monitoring 95
mediation 73
memorandum-of-agreement (MOA) 30
mentors 3, 73–74, 130
metrics 31
mistakes 68, 120
money basics 29–36
monthly capacity planning 50
morals 53, 55

Nilsson, Katarina 137–138
"no" 82, 87–88
"numbers people" 29

openness 74
organic growth 25–26
outbox delay 60
outcome, focus on 114
out-of-pocket (OOP) expenses 32
overservicing 46, 48

personal brand 5–6
personal branding 113–117
personal connections/introductions 17
personal relationships 92–96
persuasion 80–83
Picasso, Pablo 9
pitch 19, 24, 45–46
planning for future 130
praise 81, 123, 129
preparation 74, 115
privately held companies 9
procurement roadshows 17
progression **12**
project scope 30–31
proofreading 58–60
publicly traded companies 9
Public Relations Society of America (PRSA) 54, 92, 93, 134

quality control 60
questions: asking 74; open-ended 81, 82, 130

Ramsey, Dave 37
rapport, building 133–134
realistic goals 122
regional leader 13, 46
reliability 68–69
reporting lines **12**
reputation 53–54, 95
requests for information (RFI) 16–18
requests for proposal (RFP) 18–24, **20–23**
retainer billing model 32
Rockland, Alana 125–126
role definition **12**

Sandberg, Sheryl 67, 120
scope of work (SOW) 30, 38, 38–39
self-talk, positive 73
Sellers, Pattie 120
Shaw, George Bernard 86

skillsets, team building and 101–102, **102–103**
SMART goals model 121, 130
smiles 116
specialists 13, 46
specific goals 121
spellcheck 59
staff allocation plan 50
staffing 45–52, **47**
staff mix 45
"study" stage 122–123
success, understanding of 31
"sweat" stage 123
Swindoll, Charles R. 133

TalentSmart 75
team building 38, 101–110
team management 109–110
team meetings 109
team structure 13
teamwork 3, 141–142
time-bound goals 122
timelines 31
title hierarchies 9–12, *11*, **12**, 37–42
Topalanchik, Meredith 51–52
"Torches of Freedom" campaign 93
trust 54, 61, 67, 72, 74, 76, 86–87, 95, 117, 129, 133–134
Twain, Mark 53

"under-promise and over-deliver" 87
Unser, Robert 115

values, living by 76–77
Voss, Chris 82

Wilde, Oscar 72
Willis, Banks 43–44
word of mouth 17–18
work in progress (WIP) 42
writing essentials 58–63

Zinsser, William 58